One woman's work

... and other disasters

One woman's work

... and other disasters

Ruth Jennings

Matador
9 Priory Business Park
Kibworth Beauchamp
Leicester LE8 0RX, UK
Tel: (+44) 116 279 2299
Fax: (+44) 116 279 2277
Email: books@troubador.co.uk
Web: www.troubador.co.uk/matador

ISBN 978 1848767 133

Cover image by TCtoons

British Library Cataloguing in Publication Data.
A catalogue record for this book is available from the British Library.

Typeset in 11pt Sabon MT by Troubador Publishing Ltd, Leicester, UK
Printed and bound in the UK by TJ International, Padstow, Cornwall

Matador is an imprint of Troubador Publishing Ltd

MIX
Paper from
responsible sources
FSC® C013056

For family and friends

Chapter One

There is a particular publication that I would really like to trace. It will be quite a weighty tome I'm afraid. It might have *Her Majesty's Stationery Office* stamped on it somewhere. It will probably be lurking in a corner behind some reference library desk, beside the tray for the librarians' coffee cups ... it might even *be* the tray for the librarians' coffee cups. It will be called something like – *The Correlation between Early Economic and Social Conditioning, and Subsequent Gainful Employment*, and will be written by someone with lots of letters after their name. I would like to trace this publication, because I am very interested in how we all end up doing the jobs that we do.

Do frustrations with fiddly bra fastenings cause some young men to vow to design quick release fastenings, and does this lead them to becoming bra designers? Do they study hydraulics and structural engineering at university, and view page three girls with a purely professional eye, or do they just see a card in the local job centre – 'Trainee bra designer wanted' and think that the pay is OK and it's near their nan's so they could go there for lunch?

What makes some people choose to spend their lives sorting out other people's divorces, or peering into strangers' mouths, or lopping trees? Do personal circumstances matter? Perhaps if you grow up on a farm that has been in your family for six generations, and you are an only son, you are more likely to be a farmer. On the other hand, all those 5 am starts, all that mud, the sight of the vet with his arm up the bottom of your favourite cow 'Blackie' might cause you to opt for accountancy. What if your uncle leaves you a pickle factory in his will? Would you suddenly become very interested in gherkin circumference grading equipment, or see it as a means to fund your motor racing ambitions?

Anyway, what about the rest of us who don't grow up on a farm, or inherit a pickle factory, or have scarring struggles with bra fastenings? Some people do of course have talents that often appear at an early age. I doubt whether Mr and Mrs Mozart ever did worry too much about young Wolfgang ending up stacking supermarket shelves in Salzburg. The absence of supermarket shelves in Salzburg at that time would have further served to ease their concern. I don't suppose Mr and Mrs Beckham did much head scratching over David's interests either.

But what if you don't grow up on a farm, inherit a pickle factory, suffer struggles with ladies' underwear, or possess any obvious talents or skills? Mysteriously, some people just seem to know. I once asked an eight year old what he wanted to do when he grew up (there really should be a law against abusing children in this way) he said that he was going to be a doctor. Not, 'wanted to be' mind, but, 'was going to be'. But wait ... there was more. He was going to be a surgeon, and he listed what his specialities would be, and how he would attain them. Needless to say, in later life he carried out these predictions to the letter – and he wasn't even from a medical family.

But what if you don't grow up on a farm, inherit a pickle factory, write symphonies when you're three ... etc. etc. ... and don't 'just know' that you want to specialise in malfunctions of the left ventricle. We might have some vague ideas about bringing about world peace, or hope that we will become, despite indications to the contrary, so drop dead gorgeous that we will be spotted browsing through the knickers in M&S and offered a modelling contract. There is also the more recent career choice of being a 'celebrity' which of course has the added advantage of needing no talent or qualifications, other than the willingness to lead a very colourful private life, thus giving lots of copy to the tabloids, and to spending lots of time shopping for designer goods. Clearly a perfect job for some, but alas not all. And how many 'celebrities' could the rest of the workforce sustain? Could the publication that I am looking for provide the answers? I suspect that there are a lot of us unaccounted for by the above.

My own suspicion is that many of us, perhaps even the majority, with nothing to point us in any particular direction, just end up being blown hither and thither by the winds of economic necessity, opportunity, or simply chance. We end up doing a particular job because it was there and we needed the money ... or your dad knew someone who knew someone who was leaving and there was a vacancy ... or merely because it seemed like a good idea at the time. This latter reason, otherwise known as an 'ill thought out whim' seems to be becoming increasingly popular. How else can you explain why office workers, who don't speak French, and live in semis in Manchester, suddenly decide that they will convert a ruined château on the Loire into an upmarket hotel and Michelin-starred restaurant, and manage its hundred-acre vineyard? I'm not laughing. This line of 'reasoning' has featured heavily in my own job choices. Sometimes these various, arbitrary beginnings, do end up being people's jobs for life. Though not in my case.

For many years I listed between four and seven employers on my annual tax return. They were never exactly the same four to seven, and mysteriously, despite this super abundance of employment, my earnings always seemed to fall just below the taxable threshold. Yes, I know it looked suspicious, and year after year I was picked out by the Inland Revenue for special investigation. Heart sinking envelopes would plop onto my doormat, stuffed with forms full of questions like – 'Give details of your earnings between Tuesday 8th April 1959 and Thursday 19th August 1992, listing names, addresses and inside leg measurements of all employers.'

I thought that I hadn't specialised in anything, but now I realise that I have specialised in low paying part-time jobs. Year after year I spent days, weeks, phoning and writing to the Inland Revenue –

missives twanging with suppressed fury and un-shed tears, as I tried to explain that I didn't know how it happened every year, that it just did, and that I was innocent ... innocent ... I tell you! Just leave me alone and go and investigate some merchant banker, or property developer. In soothing 'dealing with crazy person' tones, they would assure me that they now understood, and had noted the singular peculiarity of my career path. But next year, back would come the forms. 'What building society interest did your husband's aunt receive between 15th July 1974 and 12th May ...' And why were there always questions about my husband's anything anyway? Pathetic though it was, this was *my* income.

Why did I have so many part-time, temporary, fleeting and clearly very low paid jobs? The truth is, I had no idea what I wanted to do. Added to this I got bored, or stressed, or both, very easily. Plus, I had the idea, which now seems quaintly old fashioned, that I should be there when my children got home from school.

I might not have known what I did want to do, but from a very early age I knew exactly what I didn't want to do; I didn't want to be self-employed. All my family were self-employed. They gathered at our house at weekends to discuss how badly they were doing. The junk shop trade was bad, the sweet shop trade was bad, and the sign writing trade was bad. I even had an aunt and uncle in Anglesey who were managing to do badly in their haberdashery shop there too. The whole family was falling apart in weekly instalments. I was terrified. I never ever wanted to be a part of this. I knew from that very early age that I wanted to hold out my hand at the end of each week (the idea of people being paid monthly was something I'd never heard of) and I wanted someone to put money into it. I would have done a good job, but what that job was, did not actually feature in this otherwise very vivid picture.

My assessment of the world of work was further strengthened by my one uncle who never complained, and who seemed to be doing rather well. He always gave me half a crown when he came to stay, and half a crown was 12½p, so he must have been doing very well. He was not self-employed; he worked for someone else, at tailoring, in Leeds. So: employed or self-employed – it seemed like no contest. Even the adrenalin rush of selling an overcoat to a non English speaking sailor, in my mother's junk shop, did not cause me to waver. I realised that I would be breaking a long family tradition of bravely running businesses that did very badly, or even the remote chance of becoming rich, but I didn't care – I did not want the terrifying responsibility. I had learned timidity from my family's boldness.

I discovered later, much later, that nobody had been doing badly at all. They were all in fact doing rather well – but heavens – you wouldn't want anyone else in the family to know that! Why? Perhaps it was just a family tradition. Perhaps it was a fear of being asked for a bob or two. I don't know.

It has occurred to me since, that if they had made it to America, which in the early 1900s was where my grandparents were heading, things might have been very different. Americans do not seem to share the English tendency to embrace and celebrate failure, nor our fear of people knowing your income. They seem happy to be successful, and eager to share this happiness. Surely family get-togethers would have been cheery and positive. However this possibility was nipped in the bud by my grandfather's chance encounter in Liverpool with an acquaintance from his small home town on the Russian/Polish border. The upshot was that Liverpool was so wonderful that there was really no need to continue to America – and that was that. By such arbitrary coincidences are our destinies shaped. My grandfather had gone ahead of the family, and he then sent a message back:

"Come quickly or I will have to go into the attic." You can't get much more cryptic than that. My grandmother, having no idea what this meant but sensing that it must be something serious, was galvanised to leave her home and everything they owned, and set off across Europe with three small children in tow, to join him. I suspect that having secured rooms for his family, he couldn't hold on to them if they didn't arrive soon, and would have been relegated to bachelor accommodation in the attic, but in those heartbreaking times you could have been forgiven for thinking the worst.

I do wonder what would make me, with or without three small children, just close the door on my house and everything in it, and walk away. Thank goodness she had the guts to do it. Most of the ten thousand of the Jewish population of that small town were wiped out.

They had owned a mill. Sometime after the war she received a communication to say that she could come and repossess it. She told them in effect (her English translations were never too good) what they could do with the mill and where they could put it, and that nothing would persuade her to set foot in their accursed country again. Well I hope that she phrased it something like that. She and I didn't get on too well on account of the shortness of my gym slip, and my bad Radio Luxembourg listening habit. I've got a nasty feeling that I would have gone creeping back to sell the property and scurry home with the money. Good for granny! I didn't appreciate her constant glaring disapproval then, but I sure appreciate her guts now – after all I wouldn't be here if she hadn't been so brave.

I could now fly for a few pounds to Poland from my local airport. Who could have imagined then, our new go anywhere, know everything world?

My grandmother, still thinking she was en route to America, but having no idea what America was going to be like, was advised, by the equally ignorant, that America was very hot, and that she wouldn't need her fur coat, so left it behind. New York ladies of a certain age, seem very fond of long fur coats. Do they all have an ancestor who left their fur coat behind when faced with the prospect of tropical capitalist climes?

So, would the American style 'you won't believe how well I did last week' have had the same effect on me? Scaredy-cat that I was, I think it might. Perhaps that is why I have been pushing myself into bizarre work challenges ever since.

But surely there was careers advice? Well, yes there was. Careers advice in the '50s for a girl in the newly free grammar schools was – teacher. If you really didn't want to be a teacher, I think nurse or secretary were also on offer, but that was it. I didn't really, hand on heart, want to do any of those things. But it didn't occur to me that there were any other jobs that I might want to do, or that might be open to me, certainly not for a working class girl. The combination of being a female and working class was bad, that much I knew.

It's difficult to get your head round now, how isolated you could be in those days, with no television or internet to give you a window on the world. You only knew what you saw around you. What would you want a career for anyway? You were only going to get married, have children, and then you would stay at home. Some employers in those days still required this of married women, with or without children. My friends' mothers were either full-time housewives, or earned pin money with a 'little job'.

My own mother forced by circumstances to support herself and me, was quite exceptional. Showing enormous enterprise, her only previous work experience having been wrapping parcels, she rented a shop, went to some auctions, and set about selling anything and everything. An offshoot of this enterprise was that everything in our house, and almost everything that I possessed, was second-hand – and yes my sister is called Rose. In later years this experience was to cause me to turn my back on barley twist legs, inlaid chests of drawers, Queen Anne chairs, and fulfil my dreams with ...teak, teak, teak ... and chipboard. If any other mothers had 'proper' jobs it wasn't talked about. So unless you knew something different – teacher, nurse, secretary, it was.

My best friend did know something different. She had an uncle in the airline industry, and told a bemused careers advisor that she wanted to be an air-hostess. An air-hostess! What was that? Alarm and horror must have swept through the spinsters of the staff room. The word was never said, but to them, 'prostitute' probably hung heavily about her choice. I don't think she was ever spoken to on the subject again. Heavens! They were there to advise weren't they? They could at least have given her some advice on contraception, or the phone numbers of some homes for fallen women.

I settled, I'm rather ashamed to say, given the aforementioned lack of enthusiasm, for teaching. My brother, the family brains, advised me in that charming way brothers can have, that I was too stupid to go to university, and that I might just about manage to hang on by my fingertips at a teacher training college. It didn't occur to me at the time, that as I had managed to pass the eleven plus, and was in the top half of the 'A' stream at grammar school, I couldn't be all that stupid. After all, he was male, and thirteen years older than me – he must be right. I knew nobody who had ever been to university, so how was I to know how clever you needed to be. It sounded very, well … 'not for people like me.' These were the days when 'not for people like me' loomed large. We knew our place!

At fifteen, some school friends and I went on a walking holiday in the Lake District. We walked between the youth hostels, on the roads, because we thought that the footpath signs were for 'real' walkers – not people like us. Whatever criticism you can level at television or the internet, or the flood of books and magazines about everything under the sun, surely nobody could be so pathetically unaware now.

Why didn't I consider a job involving either of the two things that really interested me even then: travel and gardening? Like sex, travel and gardening weren't invented until much later. Obviously some people did travel, but again, not people like us. My air-hostess friend hostessed the 'other' sort of people – real people, she even accompanied the Queen, no less! There was certainly no 'travel industry' that I was aware of – no travel agents, no travel brochures. Ordinary people did not travel abroad. Nor was there a garden industry – no garden centres, seed catalogues, gardening supplements in newspapers. Mainly because, on the whole, ordinary townies had neither gardens, nor spare money, nor time for such leisure pursuits. Our terraced house had, like most others that I knew, a wall a few feet to the front with a privet hedge. We also had one London pride plant by the front door. At the back, again like many others, we had a concrete yard with an L shaped strip of dirt. Ours was home to a horseradish plant. Some of my more upmarket friends boasted a bit of grass, but that was it. None of my family was in the slightest bit interested in gardening. Given all this, where did my passion for gardening, which began when I was about nine, come from? I can only think that it must have been some long dormant Russian peasant gene, plus the influence of my Enid Blyton 'Round the Year' book – a publication that had an enormous influence on me. I grew mustard and cress on blotting paper, and peas on rounds of cork floating in a jam jar, made weather charts, and even hunted hopefully, for the tracks of hares and foxes in the snow between the terraced houses. Russian genes and Enid Blyton – a potent combination obviously.

I was mad about growing things. The highlight of my year was the trip to Woolworths each spring, to spend hours reading the backs of all the seed packets, and coming home with enough to furnish three acres. Even the disappointments: the exotic sounding calendula that turned out to be marigolds, the fact that nothing grew well in the cat scratched dirt, didn't deter me. There was always next year – I was hooked. I suppose horticulture existed, but not anywhere near where I lived. Actually that is not quite true. There were market gardens on the outskirts of the town. But outskirts of the town … horticulture, both were way outside my world view.

Chapter Two

My brother's assessment of my potential abilities was rather borne out by my very first brush with paid employment. I was sixteen and still at school. This was a holiday job. If only I could have foreseen that the chaos and anxiety of that first work experience was going to form a recurring motif for the rest of my working life.

The job seemed simple enough. I was to sell ice cream from a kiosk in the funfair that was part of The Tower Ballroom complex in New Brighton, a seaside destination and resort in those days. The Tower Ballroom has long since burned down, and the scene of my initiation into the workplace has been soothingly grassed over. Memories are not so easy to erase.

Well, what could go wrong? I knew the difference between a choc-ice and a wafer. I could handle money in the required small amounts. It should be simple and straightforward, surely?

I turned up; twin kiss curls in place, white overall cinched by currently fashionable four inch wide black elastic belt with interlocking metal closer. I was ready to launch myself into the world of work. This is where I discovered that things are not always as simple as they might seem.

I was to start on the Easter bank holiday. Unusually, and unfortunately for me, that particular Easter bank holiday was a scorcher. Unfortunately too, little thought had been given to the design of the ice cream kiosk. It was like all the others around it – an octagonal, open-sided affair, with the freezer and till in the middle. Sensible, it seemed at first, for keeping stray fingers out of both. And all around people were happily lobbing balls at centrally placed skittles, and guessing the weight of centrally placed teddies. I have only the vaguest idea though of what was going on at the other stalls. I was stranded in the nightmare of my own.

The trouble was that people gathered to be served on all eight sides. No problem if you are selling the resistible opportunity to lob balls at something or other, but a recipe for chaos on a hot bank holiday, when you are the only source of ice cream for miles around. Crowds built up two and three deep on all eight sides. My attempts to organise them into a queue failed. My hysterical cries of, "I'm only serving from this side" failed.

Ripostes that could only have come from Liverpudlians fresh from the ferry began to fly back and forth across my lonely enclosure. Intimations that they might be quicker getting the ferry back to their place of domicile and purchasing ice cream from the shop on the corner of Paradise Street. That their ninety year old bedridden relatives could do a better job than I was doing. That old age would be theirs too, before I got round to serving them, and I would be personally responsible for them dying, three deep around my counters, of dehydration and heat stroke. That a blind and half-witted person could see that they had been there before the bastard that I was currently serving.

After a while, with that British sense of fair play, and that particularly scouse fondness for a victim (I hesitate to write derogatory things about scousers, after all I don't want to have to go and apologise, do I? But born within a stone's throw of both cathedrals – I'm a scouser too – I'll risk it) a backlash began.

"The girl's doing her best."

"Could you do better you gob-shite?"

...and the self evident –

"She's only got one pair of hands."

In the middle of this nightmare my current, actually my first, boyfriend turned up. He was a keen photographer and saw this perhaps as an opportunity to take some gritty photojournalistic shots of – young woman at work, or possibly – object of desire with kiss curls and waist clincher. I didn't need this. How could I keep up the femme fatale role that I had mapped out for myself in this relationship, in this situation?

I frantically signalled – go away. He smiled and clicked from various positions in the mob. Strangely, the one photo that I have from that weekend from hell shows me looking cool and serene. I was to remember this in my last job, on a cruise ship. Often as I was panicking about whether someone would needed repatriating – dare I ask where their insurance papers were as they lay writhing on the ground, or what was I going to do about the missing passport/priceless jewellery/husband etc? People often used to comment,

"You always deal so calmly with problems." Who, me? I didn't get it. Perhaps I should have gone in for acting.

Back at the ice cream kiosk, another necessity was surfacing. The necessity to be much better at maths than my current, 'very bad at maths' position. I don't think that I had learned the:

"So that will be 2d" (yes, old 2d bought an ice cream in those days, pre decimalisation, pre inflation, pre oatmeal and kiwi fruit Ben and Jerry's) ..."2d, 3d, 4d, 5d, 6d – your change madam." I was still at the 2d from 6d in your head, level of mathematical competence.

Well, 2d from 6d – no big deal, you might think. But these were big families. Serried ranks of little girls in satin 'best' frocks, with frills filled with sand. Little lads in hand-me-down trousers with creases down the fronts, belts scrunching them into 'can't fall down' mode. Families did still take the ferry from Liverpool to New Brighton for annual holidays as well as days out, in those 'pre fly to Spain' days. Orders were not simple:

"A choc-ice, two pink lollies ... what do you want Teresa ?...a green lolly, a wafer, two tubs, and a cornet."

I'd take the proffered two shillings with frozen fingers, and sweaty armpits – adding up and subtracting from two shillings quickly – oooh dear. Funnily enough, although I heard many,

"Eh love, I gave you a shilling, and you've only given me 4d change." I never did seem to give anyone too much change – funny that.

Chapter Three

My heart sinks as I look at my 'career' job – teaching. If only the politicians and 'experts' could choose some other football to kick around, but education is so easy. You can propose any theory you like. By the time it has been seen not to work, you have long since gone whistling into the sunset, and there is an opportunity for a new set of politicians and experts to 'correct' your mistakes. I started off enthusiastically enough.

'Cuisenaire rods' – great. I wasn't quite sure why I was bothering to teach a child that two blue bits of wood made a red bit of wood, or was it two red bits of wood made a blue bit of wood? Clearly at some point they would also have to learn that one and one equalled two. So now they would have two things to learn instead of one. But perhaps it would help them to understand, and the experts had decreed that it was a good idea, so for a couple of years that's what we all did. Then – put the Cuisenaire rods away – a new good idea had surfaced. Don't ask me what it was, I quickly stopped remembering. Funnily enough, forty years later Cuisenaire rods were back in fashion.

Comprehensive schools seemed a great idea too, despite the leg up that I, as a working class child, had derived from attending a grammar school. The experts must know what they are doing, surely. I remember well, the round-eyed amazement with which I viewed one of the first comprehensives. The lavishly equipped science labs, the music hall with a full orchestra of instruments laid out there on the floor – fabulous facilities, and of course the bright, keen, youngsters would encourage and inspire those who were less so, wouldn't they?

I saw this heady, wonderful dream of the future, in Coventry, where I attended what was then a teacher training college. Physically it was a group of old huts left over from something or other, but to me it was heaven, away from home and in swinging Coventry. I use 'swinging' as in sixties, rather than sex industry. If this sounds an unlikely description of Coventry – things were very different then. Because of the severity of its war damage it was being largely rebuilt. It had a controversial and trendy new cathedral. The country's first traffic-free shopping centre – well you had to start and make all the mistakes somewhere – and who wanted all those old-fashioned shops, and buildings, and winding roads – bring on the lovely modern concrete, and new fangled ring roads. The Queen came and opened things. The car industry was booming.

Coming from a depressed, soon to be even more depressed, Merseyside, where the shipping boom was sliding into the shipping slump, this was heady stuff. The Liverpool lads working on the docks had smuggled out oranges and bananas under their jumpers … shoes … anything.

Joke – a docker kept being stopped by the dock police but they could never find anything stolen in his wheelbarrow – he was pinching wheelbarrows.

No joke – in an attempt to stop the theft of shoes, shippers took to shipping them in batches of one foot only, in the hope that the right shoe un-loaders would be having their half shift in the pub when the left shoes arrived. ('Working the Welt' as this, 'division of labour' was known.)

This wholesale culture of pilfering gave rise to the expression 'diesel goods' as in 'diesel do for me mam, diesel do for our Tracey'. Could these two practices have hastened the transformation of so many of the dock buildings into upmarket apartments, shopping parades and museums, I wonder?

In Coventry the local lads smuggled pieces of car out under

their jumpers, to be reassembled at leisure at home. They had cars, albeit slightly mongrel looking, but cars nevertheless, and money, the car factories paid well. I had money too. I could scarcely believe why the government with such huge generosity would actually give me a grant, and let me live, learn, and eat, free, in order to have such a good time, and end up doing a 'good' – as in not selling overcoats to sailors in dockside junk shops – job. A job which would be well paid too; I started on £300 a year no less. Who could ask for more? I was blessed. I realise that this might make me sound grabby; £300 per annum, boys with cars – wooo! It wasn't really that. It was just wonderful to be, admittedly young, and free and somewhere moving forward, buoyant and optimistic. I actually live in the same area now. The last of the car factories are closing – perhaps it is my fault. Recession seems to follow me around. How did I end up back here? My husband when applying for jobs had an opportunity to take one in Coventry. Go for it, I said dreamily – it's a great place. In digs in central Coventry during a particularly wet winter in the '70s, he somehow failed to see my vision of the fabulous, fun filled, sun filled place that I remembered. It wasn't just that Coventry had changed in those twenty years – I had sent him back to my youth. That was never going to work.

But hey! There I was out in the world. Funny how just getting more central and moving away from a place where you were literally, physically squashed in a corner, was liberating. I could even go to London! Not that I did, but the prospect hovered intoxicatingly. Truth was that I had rather painful memories of my second visit to London. The first had been great, a school trip to the Festival of Britain in 1951. The second was to attend an interview at Barnet Teacher Training College. This involved a crack of dawn start – walk to the bus stop – bus to the railway station – change trains in Birkenhead – train to London, changing at Reading – get across London – train to Barnet – bus to the college.

First question:

"We see that you have put infant or junior on your application form. Do you have any preference?"

"Yes – juniors."

"… and why is that?"

"Well, teaching infants is just glorified baby-sitting, isn't it?"

Walk – bus – train back to London – cross London – Birkenhead, changing at Reading – Wallasey – bus – home.

The fact that I knew that this was a stupid, not to say ridiculous thing to say as soon as the words had left my mouth, helped not at all. Reliable engagement of brain before opening mouth is something that has continued to elude me. At least I saved Barnet from a debilitating recession.

I travelled to and from Coventry by train too. No parental to-ing and fro-ing. No parental car for a start, and only one non-driving parent. How did we do it? How did we get all our possessions back and forth? Well, we didn't have personal and complicated sound systems for a start. Have iPods meant that students can carry their own stuff? But what about toasters, electric kettles, exercise equipment, bicycles, fifty cuddly toys, TVs, cellos and five pairs of designer trainers? Our lives were not complicated by those either. My possessions were transported in a large trunk – yes, from the junk shop. I still have it – not one to throw things out much. I'd lined it with a copy of the Liverpool Echo – sophisticated eh? But it saved this gem for posterity. How's this for clear foresight? Among the ads for, 'Nylon frocks, with under-slip, feminine' 49/11d. RAF boiler-suits 26/6d. The adventures of Curly Wee and Gussie Goose, and the announcements that Crosby ambulances were to get radios, and ships were to be guided in by gas buoys, was this chat column observation:

"Rock-'n-Roll ! What the hell it's all about I don't know. But one thing I do know – it won't last.

Then there's this fella – Tommy something – Steele is it? I dare say he's a nice young man, but nobody would have listened to him in the good old days."

This was dated May 16th 1958, a couple of years before Liverpool burst on the scene as the rock and roll centre of the world. Even Tommy Steele is still going strong as I write.

I wonder whether the writer lived long enough to do the necessary writhing in agony over this 'Barnet' moment. Did he flee to the Outer Hebrides and live out his miserable life with cotton wool stuffed in his ears? Perhaps he went mercifully deaf. I hope so for his sake.

I had chosen to study pottery and natural science at college. Specifically because they had no relation to the history, English literature, and art, that had me glassy-eyed with boredom in my last years at school. This was mainly the fault of myself, and the history. I had chosen history despite the fact that history held no interest for me whatsoever and I was totally ignorant on the subject. My, 'logic' was as follows – some things like science, maths etc. you had to understand, while history you could just learn, and regurgitate. Although the words were not spoken, the Barnet curse of wrong thinking was clearly a lusty infant, even years before. I got my comeuppance on turning over the 'A' level exam paper – only two questions related to anything that I had learned – well you can't learn everything in history, can you? And due to the aforementioned lack of interest in the subject, I hadn't a clue beyond those two. Funnily enough – I nearly passed.

Mind you, I was wise to reject maths, I had had a nasty experience there too. Asked a question by the terrifying maths teacher – those were the days when teachers were allowed to be terrifying – I had decided with my aforementioned wisdom that as I couldn't answer, I would just faint instead. She'd be sorry. Unfortunately fainting took a long time to come – in fact it didn't come at all. So I just stood patiently waiting, eliciting the query as to whether I had turned to a pillar of salt like Lot's wife. This is one of the few biblical references that I remember. The pillar of salt was indelibly burned into my memory, unlike any of the maths that must surely have accompanied it. Can a pillar of salt be burned into memory? My sciences weren't up to much either.

On the subject of maths, terror, and learning – great bedfellows surely – I am really, really, good at my twelve times table. For youngsters who might not understand the concept, this is not

Ikea's new fold-out, multi-surfaced, coffee/computer/video table, but something that goes, "once twelve is twelve, two twelves are twenty four." This chant was taught surreptitiously by some of us, when the coast was clear, during the days of table prohibition. I know my twelve times table very well because when I was nine, another terrifying maths teacher (were they clones or was it that I wasn't very good at maths?) took me by the throat, pulled my face right up to her ancient, probably thirty five year old, grimacing features, and said,

"If you don't know this table by tomorrow…"

My mind has blocked out what exactly the threat was. Probably, head on a spike in the assembly hall – teachers could do such things in those days. Anyway, feet off the ground, without the 'try fainting option' – I learned it – I learned it well. I am not of course recommending the terror and heads on a spike method of teaching, but part of me does recall wistfully, that it got things done.

After two years at college, learning how to translate the returning to hive dance of the bee, a speciality of the natural science teacher, making pottery whistles, and embroidered jewel boxes, but mysteriously nothing at all about how to teach (the throw you into the classroom and then see how you got on, method was favoured at that time) I had my diploma.

I listened to my mother's pleas, and returned home to start my teaching career. To be honest I wasn't an inspired or inspiring teacher – the sort that children remember as having set them on the road to Nobel prize-winning anything, or a lifetime's interest in marine biology, or setting up schools in Mongolia. But it was a rare child who left my class unable to read, or manage basic (like mine) maths. I must have spent millions of hours fighting off sleep as thousands of children droned through, 'Janet and John' … 'Run Nip, run … Janet, see Nip run … John see Nip run … John can see Janet, Janet can see John … John and Janet can see Nip run…' Oh dear, my eyelids are drooping at the memory. Still we all have to start somewhere, and if you can read you can tackle anything, and if you can't you will be struggling for the rest of your life. I thought it was worth the daily battles with Morpheus. Plus I never put any child's head on a spike in the assembly hall, though it was a close call with some.

In those days, the '50s and early '60s, we mainly just got on with teaching the three 'R's. Children faced the front, the blackboard was used, stamps rather than drugs were exchanged in the playground, and legible writing and correct spelling were expected. Nobody told me to 'f' off or threw chairs, or threatened me with knives, and nor did their parents. We used what came to be regarded over the following years as 'old fashioned' methods, and were subsequently discarded. I have sat grumpily through those remaining years snarling at the TV news, and stabbing my finger at the newspaper, as many of the things which were routine then, are later 'rediscovered,' as they regularly are.

Where does the flood of unworkable, temporary, just short of loony ideas come from? The time consuming mountains of paperwork? The constant changes and endless stream of tests to work towards and fit in? The additions to the curriculum of so many 'extra' subjects that there is barely time for the basics. Where do they come from? Well not from any of the exasperated staff rooms that I've been in. They come from on high – the experts: government committees, policy groups, think tanks, research bodies. People that you suspect spend more time round large peaceful tables than actually teaching children. You suspect also that some of the weirder decisions are made in response to the latest sensational media revelation.

'33% of 14 year olds cannot tie own shoelaces.' Cue – compulsory shoelace tying lessons.

'64% of obese 15 year olds cannot read ingredients on baked bean tins.' Food label reading classes.

Then there are the politically correct, and planning for the future decisions.

'All 5 year olds to be offered choice of Mandarin or Swahili.'

'Lessons for all 11 year olds in filling out benefit claim forms.'

Perhaps these could replace, 'dangerous' running about in the playground time, where the competitive and potentially lethal playing of conkers might be a temptation.

Where will it all end?

'Shock revelation! 54% of school leavers deprived of places at university by inability to write their own name. School leaving age to be raised to 26.'

Probably ... and before you ask – '15,000 new truancy regulatory operatives to be recruited.'

During the snowstorm of such barmy rulings brought in during the reign of New Labour, we were only a snowflake away. But hey – what do I know? I haven't studied the subject, only the returning to the hive dance of the bee, and a history of pottery handles. I never did sit round large tables or attend conferences in exotic out of the way places. It's just that by actually doing something you see that some things work better than others, even if they did seem a good idea after a large lunch, on a Friday afternoon, at the Department of Education.

Take an example. 'Children should learn at their own pace.' Of course they should – can't argue with that. But how to bring that about? The old fashioned way – no doubt now the new or soon to be new way – was this.

When starting a new subject, say division, you talked about it and explained the general principle at length to the whole class, using the blackboard. Yes its official, I saw it on the news; blackboard usage which has been out of fashion for years, is now back in fashion. Though now I think it's a white board. Is this political correctness? Will we get brown boards? Green environmentally friendly boards, manufactured by companies run by single mothers, in deprived areas? Or as I've just seen – huge computer screen/boards. Anyway, using your old-fashioned blackboard, you set the class something to do. While the ones who had grasped what you were saying, got on, you had time to help those who hadn't. When the quickest had finished, you had some harder examples ready for them. The bulk of your time could thus be spent helping the children who needed extra help.

However, after a few years, this was considered to be 'old-fashioned,' and a new system was to be used. Everyone works at their own pace from a book, and comes to teacher to get a personal explanation when they encounter something new. It sounded good. This is how it worked in practice: quickest child gets to division and gets a long explanation from teacher while the rest of the class hopefully keep noses in books. Second quickest child gets to division – long individual explanation from teacher, while rest of class hopefully get on, except slower ones are losing interest, or have got stuck and teacher really hasn't got time to help, as queue is beginning to form for explanation of division. The length of the explanation shortens, in direct inverse proportion to its need to lengthen, as you work your way through 35 children. Plus of course the quickest are now waiting for an explanation about long multiplication. It might have seemed a good idea around that conference table at The Department of Education, but it didn't work, especially as it had been decided around some other conference table that unstreamed classes were best. I'm sure in theory they are, but the average teacher is by definition, average, and doing the best minute by minute for 35 individual children ranging from educationally subnormal to IQ 150 + might have seem possible from base camp but not to those sweating it out at the cliff face.

I think 'internal streaming' has now crept back into schools, along with smaller classes, and much needed 'classroom helpers'.

'Selection' of course is still a word to be avoided. My issue with the 11+ 'scholarship' that was used in the '40s and '50s is not one of selection in the broader sense, but the recently revealed information that girls had to achieve higher marks to pass than boys, otherwise, bright girls would have outnumbered boys in the grammar schools. I am angry, because this was the very time that girls were being told that they were not as clever as boys, except at baking, sewing, and staying at home.

My teaching career, later, also threw up another problem: teaching in the school that your own children attend. Previously, as a teacher, children's revelations about their parents had seemed so amusing.

'My mother – my mother has hair under her arms.' Well we all do, but you don't really want that shared with teacher, especially when 'arms' has been spelt – 'hams'.

Then there were the revelations of marital disharmony. The gift bearing 'uncle' who came when daddy was away, or 'we were going to go to the beach but we didn't because mum and dad had a big row,' and a multitude of other things revealed in 'news' that you really wouldn't want revealed. Sometimes it was hard to meet a parent's eyes.

Any sniggering that I may have done at other people's expense was quickly paid for.

"Your son!" Bag containing wet underpants thrust into my hands by teacher, whose playtime break had been spent mopping up puddle by her desk. Well she was kinda scary. Perhaps he had been trying to faint, and had peed instead.

Embarrassing revelations were reported with gusto.

"Non of these socks can be mine – mine have all got holes in."

"My holiday was when we went to Wigan." We were rather hard up at the time, but a day in Wigan (husband temping there), when everyone else had been to France or Italy did sound pretty pathetic.

"What I do in my spare time – I just watch TV." This last had the added twist that it was delivered publicly in assembly, to the accompaniment of a lot of teachers' fingers waggling in my direction. Why is it that children's memories are so selective? A friend told me how meticulous she had always been to keep her promises as her daughter was growing up, only to be told by her disgruntled adult daughter, that she had once promised to buy her a pair of frilly socks like the girl next door had, and she hadn't done it. A million kept promises – forgotten.

My exit from full time teaching came when I was told by his teacher that one of my own children was falling behind with his reading. After a day listening to other people's children read, I hadn't got the stomach, or the eyelid control to listen to my own much. Also I realised that I had spent my whole life in education – my own, or others. I felt the need to spend more time in the grown up world.

My exit, years later, from part time teaching came as I staggered out of a comprehensive school thinking that I'd rather clean the streets than face that any more – in fact I'd rather walk the streets, and no, I didn't mean that I would have preferred a career as an air hostess.

That was then, I hope things are better now. But I am not too confident. Ninety percent of my friends seem to have been in education in one capacity or another. Recently one of the last of them to still be actually teaching, was telling a group of us that she was about to throw in the towel. There were many problems – still sadly the ones that I have listed from years before, but one of the worst was trying to deal with disruptive pupils. There were several of them in her class with various educational, emotional, or home problems.

"Isn't there anything that you can do with them?" we asked sympathetically.

"You can send them out, there's a room you can send them to where there's a TA, but it doesn't really solve anything."

"TA?" queried the one non ex-teacher.

"Teacher's assistant," we said.

"Oh," she said, "I thought you meant Territorial Army."

We all agreed that a unit from the Territorial Army was probably a more suitable option.

Our teacher friend also told us, with some bitterness, that a recent government inspector had criticised her in his report, for not telling the children how much she was enjoying teaching them.

"Why would I?" she said, "I'm not a liar."

Quite.

Chapter Four

I had duly followed the path set out for me: married, lived in furnished rooms, worked, saved, moved up to an unfurnished flat, worked, saved and finally bought a two bedroom bungalow. Where? We didn't initially know. We had seen it from an aunt's car and fallen in love with it. It turned out to be a long way from where either of us worked and it was a whopping £3,200 – £200 beyond our wildest dreams. Added to my £300 per annum as a teacher, my husband was earning £400 a year as a Customs and Excise Officer, and in those days government jobs were the, 'good' jobs. You wouldn't want to be working in the private sector. Oh dear me no! We finally got the crippling £200 removed by desperate vendors and moved in.

We had very little in the way of furniture, no luxury items certainly, and no car. But in those days you didn't expect to start off with everything. My husband spent months renovating an ancient motor bike. The first time we took it out, the engine blew up. More months were spent working on it. Its copybook was further and fatally blotted when it broke down at the lights in the middle of the Mersey tunnel. I had to get out of the dilapidated side-car and stand, pregnant, half eaten rum-baba in hand, while my husband rummaged for tools under the side-car seat. The lights changed; we proceeded with broken clutch cable held with pliers. Worked, saved, bought a new Ford Anglia car, for £420. Figures so far have been mentioned to elicit cries of – 'How cheap everything was then!' albeit how little we earned too. But that bottom of the range car, bought at a discount because a relative worked at Fords, cost more than my husband's annual salary in a reasonably well paid job. So actually ... how cheap cars are ... now!

Worked, saved ... and had our first baby.

How quaint it seems today, the idea of getting married, a roof over your head and some money together before having the baby. Who would think of such an idea now? Who would you have for bridesmaids and page-boys for a start? As I had hepatitis along with the baby, I would have even had a great wedding colour scheme – yellow. I can picture it now – baby in yellow satin knickerbockers and frilly shirt; my matching bouquet of yellow roses. Too late now. Anyway, having your baby before the wedding was a seriously bad idea in the '50s, and all too easy, with precious little sex education; and contraceptives, or even contraception advice not available to the unmarried, certainly not where I lived. There was no legal abortion option, no welfare support for unmarried mothers, mortifying shame all round, incarceration in secret mother and baby homes, forced adoptions ... no, a seriously bad idea.

We worked some more. I split some teaching with another young mother with a baby, taking it in turns to look after the two children. We saved some more, and moved to a four bedroom house on a new estate ... and had our second child. Heavens, I could have starred in a government information film – 'What society expects of you – play the game – do it right!'

We never did manage the two point five children though. Point five is kinda difficult. But so far I had lived my life on the, 'you don't want your head on a pole in the assembly hall,' principle.

Even before marriage I had conscientiously prepared for my housewifely duties. Having attained no domestic skills from my unusually and spectacularly undomesticated mother, and fearing that my husband was not going to thrive on a diet of solely rock buns (the only thing I remembered from school cookery classes) I enrolled at evening, cookery classes. Well, yes, there was the raised hot water pastry, so useful that it was never raised again, but I did learn a lot about cheap cuts of meat, and the many, many things a girl can do with mince. Sitting on the homeward bus at night, your thighs being mottled by a hot pie, or steaming casserole, was embarrassing. Sometimes the future beneficiary of my diligence, picked up my culinary creations, and me. He had a car in those affluent bachelor days. We would drive down to the promenade, park in some secluded spot and eat whatever I had made. Who would have guessed that what was going on in that car ... the one with the steamed up windows, was ... casserole eating?

I had even toed the line on my wedding day, and not just in the area of extraneous page boys. My husband-to-be, being kind and thoughtful, was concerned that if I didn't have a white wedding, to which incidentally I was entitled, I might pine for what I had missed at some later date. Clearly he didn't know me very well, but then neither did I. Funnily enough 'what to wear' was a source of much anxiety on many following occasions, but not on that one. Well getting married was far too big a deal to concern yourself with what you were going to wear. We went together to C&A. I took a wedding dress off the rail – tried it on – it looked OK to me and to him, so I bought it.

My wedding day – 21st December 1959 – what a date for a mouthy, opinionated, young woman to tie the knot, ten days before the start of the swinging '60s that were to change everything.

The day itself was dark, cold, and very wet. Pouring with rain in fact. We were getting married in the gloomy, blackened town hall on the banks of the even greyer and gloomier looking than usual, Mersey. Everyone else was scurrying around, umbrellas up doing last minute Christmas shopping. Others using the town hall that day would be paying their rates, or complaining about blocked drains. And there was I: white lace dress, white satin shoes, veil held by a circlet of white silk flowers, and a large bouquet of pink roses. Blend in? You would never have noticed me! To add to this vision of the surreal, I found myself separated from the rest of my equally incongruously dressed party, in a lift going up to the registry office. Standing beside me was a girl that I knew from school. She was wearing a woollen coat and headscarf, and carrying a bulging shopping bag, with a bunch of celery sticking out of the top. The conversation went something like this:

"Oh, hello – haven't seen you for a while."

"Yeah ... how are you doing?"

"Oh, mustn't grumble ... and you?"

"Just getting married actually."

"Oh ... yes."

Who was she kidding that she hadn't noticed? Did she sometimes complain that her dustbin hadn't been emptied, wearing a white lace dress, a veil, and carrying a bouquet of pink roses?

Did I lovingly preserve my wedding dress in a box between layers of tissue paper, for some maybe future daughter? No I gave it to the little girl across the road, to cut up to make dresses for her dolls.

Fast forward twelve years and two children later, short of money and bored now, I looked for a job that fitted in with being a mother with no access to help, and one child still pre-school. I saw an advertisement for the job of, post-school/pre-supper, helper at a nearby children's convalescent home. My husband on flexitime could get home a bit early a couple of nights a week, so I could do that.

I meticulously removed traces of food from my clothing. Put together what I hoped was a not totally mumsy outfit, and presented myself for interview. The room was alarmingly full of applicants, some of them, discouragingly, were even men. My heart sank.

The tour of the home had me in a permanent mist-up. Poor little mites: limping, coughing, holding out their hands to us, sliding across the floor on their bottoms. I desperately wanted to help these children, desperately. Had I found my vocation? My eagerness obviously shone through.

The filling of the post was organised in a strange way. We were all interviewed, and then sat together in a room. After a time someone came into the room and said that I had got the job, and

...yone else hadn't. I immediately began apologising to the bemused applicants for winning.

This was a trait that was to bring approbation later in life. Having a quiet drink in a rural Welsh pub with my husband and adult sons, we were wheedled into taking part in the pub quiz, and won. Well I really did feel sorry for the local drinkers deprived of the prize of a large amount of beer, that was clearly intended for them. How were they to know when they asked the name of some obscure American airport, that one of our group was a travel agent in New York? Or that we could field experts on the two world wars, gardening, sport, pop music, computing, and real ale? Seemingly apologising in these circumstances is the wrong thing to do, and I have never lived it down.

Anyway, flushed with the heady thought that I could land a job in the face of much opposition – even male, I looked forward with huge enthusiasm to starting.

I was going to impart my love of nature to these poor mites. I would take them to the nearby seashore; together we would explore rock pools. We would make a garden in the grounds – grow vegetables. In winter we would make miniature gardens in bowls – study bird life. I would dust off my Enid Blyton 'Round the Year' book – track animals in the snow, make weather charts. Now I could see myself featuring in Nobel acceptance speeches as the inspiration for some break-though.

'Crabs are our ancestors' ... 'A cure for the common cold from the slime of the sea slug.'

A lot of the children's disabilities seemed rather modest to keep them full time in a convalescent home: diabetes, bronchitis etc. I suspected that perhaps the quality of their home life was a factor too. So it was disconcerting to say the least to realise that I had spent time as a child at this very institution, suffering from bronchitis. I didn't realise at first because I thought that I had been sent to some other country, a million miles away. The bombing of Liverpool, and my own troubled home life added weight to this theory as to why some of the children were there. Anyway, that was then, and this was now – I couldn't wait to get started.

I did wonder why my rotas always consisted of the fourteen and fifteen year olds. Still, deprived no doubt of contact with nature for even longer than the younger children, they would surely be even more astonished and grateful for my revelations.

Ready to set off for the seashore, on my first afternoon, with my group of fifteen year old boys, I passed a fellow worker with his group of fifteen year old girls.

"I don't know what they told you," he said, "but the main object of the exercise is to keep the boys and girls away from each other."

Whatever could he mean? Well my boys were going to have their captivated little heads over rock pools so whatever his problem was; it wasn't going to be mine.

Each group included one wheelchair. I quickly discovered the problem that this presented. The other boys were eager to push it. That was so caring of them I thought happily. Not so it seemed. The wheelchairs, with no resistance from their occupants were seen as a potent source of entertainment. You could mow down pedestrians, ram street furniture, push the chair suddenly onto the road, causing satisfying squealing of brakes, possibly even get a bit of a pile-up going. No, better I push the wheelchair. However, pushing the wheelchair meant that you couldn't stop the others from running ahead, snapping overhanging branches from garden trees, asking passers-by for money, and menacing any children who crossed their path. All this, I learned in the fifteen minutes that it took us to reach the beach. Still, it would be better at the beach where there would be more room for them to express themselves, I thought hopefully.

We arrived at the beach. But before I could explain the delights that were in store for them, the distant figures of buxom teenage girls appeared, scattered about in the adjacent sand hills, waving and beckoning like sirens of the sands. I gazed aghast at these busty Lorelei – this is what he had meant. Before I could utter a word, the boys had scarpered. Within seconds I was left with one

29

boy in a wheelchair, one other boy, and one large ball, brought in the unlikely event that the rock pools would fail to entrance.

What was I to do? They hadn't even had the decency, or indecency, to all head for the sand-hills. They had fanned out in all directions. The horror of having to go back and admit that I had lost almost all of them! This was a seriously huge expanse of beach, and I knew that it was subject to tricky tides. Drownings and unwanted pregnancies whirled round in my brain. By the time I had reached the conclusion that I couldn't reach a conclusion, most had disappeared from sight anyway.

Noting that the two remaining boys had struck up a friendship with two boys in open necked shirts and Enid Blyton shorts, who had come out of a house backing onto the beach, and were playing cricket with them, I decided to see if I could recapture at least a few of my lost boys. I wandered vaguely towards the sand-hills, what I would do when I got there I had no idea. I examined the faces of boys I passed on route – were they mine? I had no idea of course, I had only just set eyes on 'my' boys. And how would parents returning from buying ice creams react to an obviously distressed woman asking their children if they were hers? I didn't want to end up in a police station trying to explain myself to a psychiatrist as well. Realising the futility of my wanderings, but still no nearer to a solution I returned to the cricket game.

An altercation had broken out. The boys in the Enid Blyton shorts were accusing my boys of stealing their cricket ball. My boys were adamant that they hadn't got it. The older boy immediately sensing that my arbitration was going to be futile, went off and returned with his father; a pleasant man, also wearing an open-necked shirt, who could indeed have been Uncle Dominic in 'The Secret Seven and the Treasure of Slapton Sands.'

With more than a hint of a sob, I explained my predicament to him. He was very sympathetic. I also explained that my poor boys couldn't possibly have stolen his middle class cricket ball. How could they accuse this poor boy, who had now been cowed into returning to his wheelchair? To prove my point I whipped off the blanket covering his trembling knees ... and the cricket ball. The wheelchair occupant leapt from the chair, and the two boys ran and hobbled at speed in the direction of the sand-hills.

I remember vividly the loneliness of it. Standing there with two boys and one man in open-necked shirts, one wheelchair, two balls, and none of my charges. My stunned state of misery was interrupted by the man.

"Are those yours?" He said pointing to three specks in the distance, heading out to Hilbre Island. They were bound to be.

Hilbre Island is only an island when the tide is in. The Irish Sea rushes in cutting it off at high tide, whereas at other, 'tide out' times you could walk out across the vast expanse of sand to it. Ominously, nobody else was walking out to it now, just three boys. I reckoned they were about half a mile out.

I had a lot of experience of tides and tidal islands. As a child of nine or ten I used to run out along an exposed sewer pipe to a sandbank in the Mersey, and there amuse myself collecting shells and watching the ships go by. Of course one had to keep an eye on the tide. When it came in, it swept around the sandbank – it would cut you off – and then drown you. Often the first stealthy creepings of the tide were not obvious as I was frequently playing there at dusk, before skipping my way in the dark, around the park on my way home. Why on earth did my mother allow me to do this?

I had a wonderful Guardian cartoon strip on my wall till it yellowed and fell to pieces.

A woman turns to her mother and says:

"You were never there for me – you never cared – you just let me run wild." Her mother says,

"I did it because I wanted you to have what I didn't have." She turns to her own mother, and says,

"You stifled me, always watching me, organising me – I had no freedom, you never let me learn from my mistakes." Her mother says,

"I wanted you to have what I never had." She turns to her own mother, and says,

"You neglected me – you never cared – you let me run wild ..."

And so on down the generations to the ancient wizened mother in the wheelchair.

My mother wanted me to have the freedom that her brothers had had, but that she hadn't. And me? I opted to stay home and bake cakes on rainy days and fuss over my children.

As I now gazed at the receding figures and the advancing tide, the fact that I had survived my mother's altruistic willingness to allow me to sacrifice myself on the altar of personal freedom, did not apply. It would go down very badly in a court of law.

"You took out fifteen boys. How exactly did you come to return with one wheelchair and a beach ball?"

I would be personally responsible for the, 'Three boys drown tragedy' headlines in The Liverpool Echo. Would I also be responsible for the babies now no doubt being conceived among the sand-hills? More to the point, could the latter be proved?

It was nearly time to go back to the convalescent home. What was I to do? I do remember kindly Uncle Dominic offering to help me, but I can't remember at all what we did, or even what we could have done.

Then the miracle happened. From all directions the boys trooped back. Admittedly some were adjusting their clothing, and others appeared to be carrying things that I don't remember them carrying on the outward journey, but at the necessary departure time, they were all there.

And do you know what? They really had had an interesting and satisfying trip to the beach, not quite the one that I had planned, but they were now tired and ready for supper – that at least was the object of these outings. And Enid Blyton too, really had featured in the proceedings, though not quite as I had anticipated either. Still, children tired, fulfilled, and happy.

Me? ... I was indelibly traumatised – we were never going to the beach again – sod the rock pools. We would go to the park next time.

The park however had a large lake and hills. The favourite game in the park was to push the wheelchairs, with or without occupants, down the hills and into the lake – they all loved it – even the wheelchair occupants. As well as wheelchair games, you could push your friends, or with a bit of luck, other children into the water. There were toilets for trysts, and artistic decoration, flower beds to desecrate, dogs to torment, old people to set a tutting.

How about a walk around the golf course? Exhilarating views – goodness you could see as far as Wales. Great for bird spotting – was that a White Throated Warbler?

Wait a minute – who were those boys? The ones picking up golf balls from the greens and trying to sell them back to the golfers? They might be the same boys that I had seen coming out of the off-licence with the bottles of beer, as I toiled up the hill with the wheelchair.

When I caught myself telling some undernourished waif with one hip higher than the other so that his trousers were always at half mast, to not drink from a can in the street because it was … 'not nice' I realised that I had become too irredeemably middle class to do this job. Either too middle class … or not middle class enough … to help these boys.

Perhaps groups of teenage girls would be better – they weren't. They perhaps did less physical damage to the environment and law abiding citizens, but moved about in a cloud of poison difficult to penetrate without breathing apparatus. They fought and sulked and fell in and out of friends with each other at bewildering speed. I could find nothing, but nothing, that interested them. Diverting some of their astronomically abundant hormones to menopausal women might have worked, but was an option not open to me.

One spin off from this job was that my own children, who had seemed pretty irritating when I left them, seemed positively angelic by the time I returned home. I stuck the job out for as long as I could, which wasn't, I'm ashamed to say, very long. I tried to ease my guilty conscience by telling myself that it would give my delighted successor the opportunity to apologise to another roomful of hopefuls, for being a winner while they were losers.

Mmmm ... yes ... I think I do see now, however well it is meant – it is not a good idea.

Chapter Five

I began my door knocking days because of my previously mentioned desire to be home, and being warm and motherly, at the end of the school day. Unlike my mother who was never there for me ... etc. ... etc. I started to explore jobs in 'market research'. Doesn't that sound grand? In no way does it sound like the last resort of the desperate. My reasoning was, that you could do this job whenever you liked, and still be home putting the final pastry leaves onto that apple pie at four o'clock.

This didn't quite work out. An essential element of market research is that you need to get hold of some market initially, in order to research it. You also need a cross-section of ages and employment statuses to boot. So it stands to reason that 40-50 year old men in full time employment are unlikely to be available to be interviewed at a time of my choice: 2pm – after a light lunch and the 1 o'clock news. To save myself a lot of knocking on the doors of empty houses, I had to start at the very time that I was trying to avoid. Still, I told myself, self-reliance is valuable too, and I would be all the more appreciated when I was there, dusting the Lego.

I think that I worked for more than one market research body, but the experience was apparently so fascinating, that I really can't remember.

One year I did help with the census. Funny how difficult it was to convince people that they had to do it; that it wasn't optional. Millions must have been spent on publicity, but I still got,

"No thanks dear, not today."

"No, I'm not bothering … I'm not interested in it."

The main bulk of my 'investigative endeavour' though, was for the Broadcasting Audience Research Board or BARB as it was, and probably still is, called. The reason I expect that I remember this job, and not the others, is that I was interested in the results. Shocking as it may seem, I really didn't care much about what brand of cereal people consumed, and could sympathise with the imposition of being made to stand in the doorway while the children maimed each other, and the spaghetti boiled over, in order to tell me whether or not they would look more favourably on peach or crème de menthe coloured toilet paper. The BBC however was important stuff. Future programming, funding, careers even might hang upon my findings.

I had wondered how those league tables of the most popular programmes were drawn up. I always had a suspicion that someone was just making them up somewhere, perhaps money changed hands, or favours were called in. I was genuinely surprised and gratified to discover that people actually went out and asked viewers and listeners what they had been viewing and listening to. I think that, even then, they were experimenting with plug-in TV monitors. Soon I suppose there will be plug in brain chips not only to monitor what you watch but also what you think of it. But certainly people like me used to go out and knock on people's doors and ask – three hundred and sixty five days a year.

The reason that I thought the results were made up, was that they were so depressing. Surely they couldn't be true. Even more depressing was to find out that they weren't made up. I used to get quite cross, inwardly of course, on days following programmes that I had enjoyed.

"No, it was boring, switched over after ten minutes."

Could that have been two minutes pea brain? Why didn't you give it a chance? Huge amounts of money were spent on it. The drama department will fold because of you, personally.

"Thank you." Smile. Next question.

I came to the sad conclusion that we get exactly what we want. Knowing this, it is even more depressing to consider the nation's current favourites; these ensure that 99% of our TV coverage is, in no particular order, as follows:

1. Millions of hours of people doing things with balls. Ditto number of hours discussing why ball did or didn't go into or over net, pole, or down hole in ground.

2. Soaps, featuring people with very, very, eventful lives.

3. Videos of people falling over or crashing into things, and hurting themselves.

4. People hanging about in human zoos, or jungles. Will they or won't they lose their tempers, or claim that the capital of England is Australia, or eat maggots?

5. Are you very: fat / thin / tall / short or having cosmetic surgery? Can we come and gawp?

6. Quizzes (studio) – get rich quick. Quizzes (phone in) – get poor quick. Just answer this question – who was the son of God? Was it – Jeremy Clarkson, Jesus Christ, or Elton John?

7. People failing at doing things e.g. DIY, controlling their children or dogs, changing their lifestyles, singing, dancing, or not looking old, or badly dressed.

8. Terrible old films, or films that you thought of fondly as good, and now see, weren't.

9. Collections of bits of things – 100 best TV farts, people saying 'bleep,' or forgetting lines.

10. People trying to run faster, jump higher, throw something further, than anyone else.

This last entry has such playground connotations that I'm surprised there are no spit furthest, pee highest categories – the Olympic committee are probably considering their inclusion at this very minute.

Apart from finding people at home, another challenge was filling age categories. I got very good at reading houses. Bedroom window – soft toys – parents probably in thirties. Bedroom window – curtains pinned together or heavy metal posters – parents probably in forties. Excessively tidy front garden with lots of bedding plants – retired couple.

Age was tricky in another way too. By the end of the day I was always looking for someone 'special' – a thirty year old woman, or fifty year old man. The door opens – you have a split second to make up your mind. After a few:

"I would like to interview a woman over sixty – do you have a few moments?" only to be told that the lady standing before me was forty five but had clearly had a hard life, I hit upon the following: I am looking for someone over fifty. Door opens. Apparently ninety year old man stands before me.

"Oh, sorry to bother you. I need to speak to someone over fifty and you clearly are not."

"Bless you dear, I'll be seventy six next birthday. What can I do for you?"

Everyone happy. It's enough to disturb people in the middle of cooking, or going to the lavatory. No need to shatter their self esteem as well.

Sometimes the research was of a more detailed nature – what people thought of BBC news coverage etc. And it was necessary to persuade people to let me into their homes and take up 20 minutes or so of their time, as well as ask impertinent questions about their job status and incomes. Well I suppose it wouldn't do to get poor people's opinions confused with rich people's opinions. It never failed to amaze me, that even with my identity card showing that I was a bona fide who I said I was, people were willing to give me so much personal information. Admittedly someone sewing 10,000 sequins onto a dance dress, or appropriately, bored with afternoon TV, often seemed glad of the diversion, and company. And I was good at keeping an eye on the baby, or volunteering that I thought the magnolia paint actually looked a better choice for the hall than the magenta. But some people let me bombard them with questions while they followed recipes, or plastered scraped knees. Bless them.

I've always been intrigued by the huge variations between people's living styles, and this gave the job an added interest. Some people live their lives with neatly ordered precision. Two coats on hall stand, clear sweep of coffee table, immaculate arm covers on couch. Next door, neighbours plough through twenty pairs of shoes, half eaten take-aways, mugs of congealed coffee, and five dogs.

Dogs – now there's a puzzle.

Ring bell. Ferocious and prolonged barking and snarling sounds from other side of door. Step back in fright as apparently hippo sized dog hurls itself at other side of flimsy door. Door judders. Unable to shoulder its way through, dog tries to scratch its way to my side of door. Do I hear sounds of splintering? Sound of approaching person, issuing instructions for dog to stop said behaviour. Dog's grizzled muzzle appears in space where letter-box has been ripped off. Dog snarls, and bares fangs. Human voice raised on other side of door.

"Stop it … get … down."

The snarling muzzle is repeatedly pulled back, and returned to aperture.

"Get down … get back … get in … there."

The muzzle disappears, but low pitched and frantic barking, accompanied by occasional high pitched yelping, continues. Dog or master periodically thump against door as struggle progresses.

"Get…in…there."

Triumph – the sound of a door slamming. Barking and clawing are at one remove now. The front door is opened –

"Yeah?"

Why on earth do people want to suffer that every time someone comes to the door? I really, really, can't understand it. But at least I was not physically involved. Worse, was the door being opened with the snarling, barking hound being held with immense difficulty by its collar, as it flings its gigantic paws onto your chest, or if it can't reach your chest, throws itself at your shins. You are rewarded then with the time-honoured,

"He won't hurt you."

My sole concern is not just about whether he will hurt me or not – I don't like it. I don't care what sort of relationship consenting adults have with their dogs behind closed doors. Just leave me out of it.

Going into strangers' houses posed another problem. Man comes to door.

"Could you answer some questions about what you watched on TV or listened to on the radio yesterday?"

"Sure dear – come in."

How can you ask – are you alone? Is your wife in? Are you an axe murderer? You really can't, and I never did solve that one satisfactorily. You could listen hard for any sounds coming from the interior, but then, that could be his partner in axe murdering, sharpening the axe. If a man answered the door and said that he was busy now but come back in half an hour, I'm afraid that I said I would, but didn't. What if he used that half hour to pop down to the local corner shop for some Rohypnol to slip into the proffered coffee? One of the safeguards, I reckoned, was that you were taking people by surprise. So apologies to any innocent man who waited in vain for my return. The fact that people were not expecting you, works two ways though. Axe murderers may not be prepared to axe murder, but they might also be caught by that ring on the bell whilst in their underpants … or less.

I was ringing bells one Saturday morning on the third floor of a block of flats. A man came to the door wearing a dressing gown. Yes, he would answer some questions, but come in. Not unnaturally he would not want to stand on the landing in his dressing gown. I couldn't get around to the 'is anyone else there' in time – no-one was. I found myself sitting opposite a man lounging on a low settee who clearly had nothing on under his dressing gown. I managed to keep my eyes fastened to his face, but I was well aware that nobody knew where I was, so that if anything happened to me, or I just disappeared, no-one would have the faintest idea where to look for me. Nothing untoward did happen. I had surprised the poor man, and he had kindly agreed to help me. Now I realise that I could have made up some rule about two people having to be present. There might even have been such a rule. Bit late to get my head round it now.

Three hundred and sixty five days of the year was no exaggeration. Christmas holiday ratings were of mega importance, but how did you get people to do this job on Christmas Day? The answer was – pay very well, beg, plead, and threaten. One year I succumbed. I would go out, earn good money, and render this vital public service, on the understanding that I was to be excused kitchen duties at home.

When was the best time to disturb someone's Christmas Day? During their morning lie-in as they slept off their Christmas Eve hangover? During the opening of the presents? In the, 'Oh my God the brussels sprouts have stuck to the pan,' period? Actually during Christmas dinner itself? During the post dinner coma? There was no good time to go into strangers' houses on Christmas Day and ask them a lot of questions about TV programmes. I just plunged in when I was ready. They were going to kill me anyway. I envisaged spending the whole day wandering about, like some middle aged Tiny Tim, peering from rainy pavements into brightly lit rooms where people were eating and drinking, wearing paper hats, and pulling crackers.

It wasn't like that at all. To my surprise and joy, everyone was so amazed and appalled that I had been sent out to do this job ... on Christmas Day for heaven's sake, that I was borne up on a warm, 'love in' of mince pies, newly opened chocolates, and enough offers of alcoholic drinks to have me ending the day in jail, or on a life support machine.

Here, there was a – "Wow – you're kidding!" There, I suspect I nipped a major family row in the bud. I was sometimes a welcome entertainment, and I reckon, a story to tell ..."Guess what happened?... and on Christmas Day!" in households where I suspect nothing much was going to happen anyway. I returned to my own Christmas, buoyed up with mince pies, the warmth of human kindness, and just a couple of small sherries.

My favourite interview? Well it wasn't the one where the door opened to mother and small child.

"This lady has come to take you away – I told you someone would come to take you away if you didn't behave." Child screams in terror. And it wasn't my very first interview on my first assignment. Nervously sticking exactly to my script, I'd followed up,

"Occupation?" with, " … and do you have any qualifications?" The dentist that I was speaking to was understandably affronted.

No, it has to be this one. Door opens to young woman. She tells me in some detail what she watched the night before – adding her opinions and highlighting her favourite bits. Man appears in doorway behind her.

"We haven't got a telly," he says firmly.

"Oh no," she says trying to look as if she has just remembered, "we haven't."

One effect that this job had on me, was to make me very sympathetic to all market researchers. Even … perhaps especially … the three fourteen year old girls, part of a school project it seemed, let loose in my local town centre:

Bit of giggling and nudging.

"Can we ask you some questions?"

"Yes."

More giggling and nudging.

"What are you doing here?"

"I live here." Consternation – something had gone wrong. Exchanged glances and squirming.

"Er … I mean what are you buying?"

"Some fruit and some liver." Discussion as to how to spell 'liver' – what was it anyway?

"Why do you shop here?"

"Because I live here."

"Oh … yes." … More squirming.

"Last question. Where do you live?"

I'm not laughing; really, I know how easy it is to do.

Years later, after I had finished doing this job, by some coincidence a BARB researcher knocked on my door. My delighted surprise in seeing her, and enthusiastic invitation to her to come in, must have rung the old axe murderer alarm buttons. I couldn't have been more willing to help. The trouble is I'm hopeless. I have no idea at what time I decided to switch on, or over, or when I decided to give that programme another try for ten minutes. Worse still I never know which channel I'm watching anyway. I do not know whether I am watching ITV or BBC news. I channel hop constantly with no mental registration at all. This is an old affliction akin to my being able to sing all the words of 'Temptation' or 'Once ... on a high and lonely hill, in the morning mist two lovers kissed ...' and yes I could go right to the end, but at the same time having no idea who recorded them, or when.

How all those thousands of people remembered all those details, beats me.

Chapter Six

I have a problem with driving.

Everyone I know drives as easily as they walk, some drive even more easily than they walk. No need to even think about it – get in car – drive – easy. Sadly though, not me. Even the friends who, against my advice, drive down my long narrow drive with its culmination into an 'impossible to turn if there is another car there' turning circle, will then happily reverse in random zig-zag fashion, oblivious to the threat they pose to my tasteful lamp post lights, walls, and herbaceous borders. They then have to back out into a busy road, often waving away my offers to help in this highly dangerous manoeuvre. Some of them bypass the 'threat' to demolish plants altogether, and just reverse straight into the middle of my herbaceous border in order to turn. The trauma of doing any of these things, unlikely I admit, as I would never have ventured down the drive in the first place, would have kept me from venturing out in the car for a year … at least. But are they bothered? No. They will have forgotten about it by the time they get home, and will be back in the car in half an hour.

I once spent a whole night lying wide awake and frozen with fear at the prospect of backing out of the position that I had got into in the car park of a b&b. In the event, with not even a wink of sleep to sustain me, I backed out first time, no trouble. Oh, yes, I can drive. The only admonition that my driving instructor ever made was to gently point out that the slow down to 20mph sign didn't actually apply to me. I was probably doing a white knuckled ten at the time.

I even passed my driving test first time. True, during the actual test I did twice run backwards on an unrecognised hill start, but the examiner said that as I had promptly dealt with the application of the brakes, he was passing me, on the understanding that prompt action to correct mistakes was just as important as not making the mistake in the first place. How wise.

I have never had an accident either. Twice people have run into me while I have been stationary at halt signs, but I personally have never even scratched the car. Scratch the car! I would rather be suspended by my thumbs from a motorway bridge. So what is my problem? I have two main areas of difficulty. First, I seem to have a quite serious lack of spatial awareness. I have only ever been required to drive a medium sized family saloon or hatchback, but to me it feels like a deluxe, three bedroom motor home ... I will never squeeze past this row of parked cars, or manage to shoe horn myself between those two cars parked thirty yards apart. I am constantly getting out of the car to check how many inches I am from the car in front, or the pavement, to find that I am five feet away. I close my eyes and grit my teeth when I am a passenger, as the driver insists on trying to park in impossibly tiny looking spaces, only to discover that there are three feet on either side. I am hopeless, and friends or husband very kindly ferry me about, or I use my bike.

Now cycling through heavy traffic scares the wits out of most of the people that I know, but bothers me not at all. I think it's logical. You can stop and put your foot down when in difficulties on a bike. Stopping and/or putting your foot down when faced with congestion in a car is not a good idea at all. The other reason that cars scare me is that they are so dangerous. No-one else seems to be quite so aware, at least not on a daily basis, that these are lethal weapons that can, and do, kill and injure thousands of people every year. I am always very conscious of the fact that one misjudged move, one mistaking one pedal for another, one wasp in the car, and you could kill yourself, or more importantly some totally innocent other person. I always say a little prayer of thanks when I arrive home safely … me safe … car safe … pedestrians that ventured out that day … safe.

So it came as a big surprise to everyone who knows me, when I took on a job that required driving up to 200 miles a day into unknown city centres to try to find unknown supermarkets, and park in their busy multi storey car parks. 'Big surprise' is actually rather an understatement. Total incomprehension fits better, with lots of, 'hows?' and 'whys?' and 'are you crazy?'

But for goodness sake, I'm a big girl. I should be able to deal with this. Heavens! my cousin Moses from Anglesey could drive. People of all ages, who are not particularly bright, or brave, or technical do it. I felt that I really needed to tackle it. I would drive, drive, drive, until like everyone else, it became just something that I did without thinking. How was I to do this? The thing is, I know myself well enough to know that if I say I will do something – I will do it. Nobody at the margarine firm that I was to work for had questioned my ability to do the necessary driving – why would they? They had no inkling that I had once proved, fortunately before I got into the car, that 'shit scared' is not just a figure of speech. But I wouldn't let them down – I knew it. The job interview, weirdly, given all this, took place in hotel room 101. The room that holds what you fear most.

The job, with the grand title of, Midlands' Supervisor but still only part time, left me with those all important – warm scones with home-made jam possibilities, on non-working days. It involved, not surprisingly, supervising all over the Midlands. What was I supervising? Well, you know when you are in a supermarket and someone dressed as a rabbit, or in an apron with a gigantic logo on it, asks if you would like to sample this new mango and coriander, fat-free, salt-free spread, and they hold out a tray of bits of cracker with stuff smeared on it? I would be supervising that.

The next question, and I asked it of myself, was why? Why did this simple seeming operation need supervising? Too much garlic and radish spread? Too little? Rabbit ears too floppy? Not floppy enough? Never mind. They wanted supervisors, and after all, I had my own agenda – becoming a fearless driver.

My first day's assignment involved two stores in Leicester which I didn't know – that's city or stores. A store in Derby … ditto, a store in Nottingham … ditto. A store somewhere on route to Birmingham, and a couple in and around Birmingham itself, which I knew well enough to know I was not going to enjoy – Spaghetti Junction – me? And how could you possibly do all of those?! Especially as the presentations didn't start till 10 am and finished at 4. Also the days used were the busy end of week ones, when traffic would be at its worst.

I remember asking someone in the car park of my first store on the outskirts of Leicester for directions to my next store in the city.

"Ooo" he said, "traffic's a nightmare on that road … I'd get the bus love."

At each store I was to sign in, speak to the manager, creep up on the demonstrator to ensure that she was in a good position and doing what she ought, speak to her, sort out any problems, and write a detailed report. I did try at one point to save time by leaving the reports to write at home – big mistake. By the time that I had got my addled brain and frayed nerves back home, I had no idea what had happened at any particular store. Was that the one where the girl had been picking her nose? Or was that the one where she had been flirting with the spotty youth on the delicatessen counter?

Needless to say, driving through unknown cities, on unknown ring roads, looking for stores when I didn't know where they were, and then finding somewhere that the nervous driver of a forty foot motor home could safely park, was every bit the nightmare that I expected. Sat Nav would have been a big help, but unfortunately it wasn't, as yet, even a glint in an inventor's eye. I coped as best I could. I made copious notes as to how to reach stores, only to find that next time, I was approaching from a different direction, as each time I had a different mixture of stores. I parked in any quiet open space that I could find, and walked the last quarter mile.

Occasionally I managed to find five adjacent parking spaces on the top floor of a multi storey car park, and managed to squeeze into that. Eventually I got a little braver and would try to squeeze into three adjacent spaces on a lower level used by normal human beings. I then frequently spent precious time examining every car on level three in Derby, before I remembered that I'd parked on level three at Nottingham, not here. Where had I parked here then?

For me it really was a nightmare job. But it wasn't all driving. There were day conferences to attend too. I could take the train for those. I could take the train to Birmingham or sometimes London. I would arrive at some large hotel, find the suite that the conference was taking place in, have a coffee and some biscuits, and then spend the morning listening to some company conference organisers reading word for word exactly what it said on the paperwork that we had already been sent for the forthcoming campaign, then pointing with a stick to a pie chart, also on paperwork sent; and then watch the six second TV ad that would be shown for this product. Buffet lunch. More reading from posted information, more pointing with stick at target figures on screen, also in posted paperwork. Break for coffee and biscuits. More reading and pointing. Then long journey home.

I have never seen the point of such meetings, and I suspect that this company was not alone. What are they for? To keep company conference planners in a job? To stop hotels from looking dead during the day? To increase consumption of custard creams? Did they suspect that we couldn't read? How did they expect illiterates to do this job anyway?

However my diligent attention to all this pointing and pointlessness must have been appreciated by my employers. I was entrusted with a special assignment of great delicacy. I was asked to make a round trip of some 150 miles to bestow a large number of cuddly toys and a grovelling apology upon a possibly traumatised customer. Said customer had discovered a condom in their tub of margarine. Delicacy on all sides prevented the touching upon of the status of the condom. I clung to the assumption that it was unused. The alternative didn't bear thinking about…

"Has this toast got a kind of funny taste … or is it just me?"

The good news was that apart from still adhering to the, 'arriving home safe prayer' I did get much more relaxed with my driving. I was even sometimes relaxed enough to prise one clawed hand from the driving wheel and put on some music to listen to on motorways. I was even sometimes relaxed enough to listen to it. My knuckles sometimes even showed a hint of pink.

The bad news was, that as soon as I stopped doing this job, I reverted almost immediately to the old terror.

Chapter Seven

Following the driving job, adrenalin must have again been lacking in my life. Too many baking sessions perhaps. That's the only reason I can see as to why I seemed to be actively seeking out 'bungee jumping' type jobs. The next one though didn't seem too scary. To be honest I didn't think carefully about it at all; it was never going to happen – I was just indulging in a bit of harmless fantasy.

I have really no idea why everyone wants to be on television these days. Saying that it is so easy to make a fool of yourself, and not just in some relatively minor way, but in front of possibly millions of people, is to totally miss the point I suppose. If you don't get to make a fool of yourself in front of millions of people, how will you ever get famous or sell your story to the tabloids. I had no ambition to do either of these things. As usual I had missed something vital. So how did I get to appear on TV?

It happened like this. Midlands TV at that time put out a gardening programme. 'Gardening Today,' it was called. One of the presenters was Cyril Fletcher, the comedian and teller of 'odd odes'. The style was very casual, lines were fluffed, corny jokes were made.

"You could do better than that," my husband commented once – not interested, but forced to watch gardening, due to our only having one television, and in the unlikely hope that I would get bored and switch over to the football.

"That's just the sort of thing you'd say," he added, after Cyril Fletcher made some squirm inducing joke. Perhaps my husband was just amusing himself with these annoying interruptions. But he did have a point. It set me thinking. In those days, the '70s, you didn't see women presenters of gardening programmes. Now there are plenty, but not then. Why, I thought? All the gardening enthusiasts that I knew were women; why shouldn't women do it?...Why shouldn't I do it?

What I didn't know about the programme, was that it was supposed to represent an expert chatting informally to an amateur – Cyril Fletcher, and that's why it had this rather off the cuff air to it ... it was being done ... off the cuff. However, undaunted by this essential but absent information, I took it upon myself to write to the programme's producer, and ask him in no uncertain terms why there were no women presenters of gardening programmes – tell him that I thought there should be – and put myself forward for the position.

Feeling that I had to put forward some justification for my forthrightness, I totally negated my worthy feminist attack, by listing some things that I thought women presenters would be good at contributing: flowers for arranging, garden colour schemes, using herbs – why didn't I go the whole hog, and include baking yummy strawberry shortcake, or making lavender filled dolly bags – and betray women totally?

Among the things that I had mentioned, was my irritation with the male obsession with growing huge vegetables. What for? I still don't understand it. Why would you want an eight foot parsnip grown in an eight foot drain-pipe, and watered from a ladder. It's too big to go in a pot, or even in the average kitchen, it's probably tough as old boots, and no, it isn't your penis, so don't bother trying to convince people that it is. Woooo – I'd have to be a lot more controlled on that subject.

To my amazement, and I have to say, more than a slight stab of horror, the nice producer wrote back and said, yes he was interested in my ideas, and particularly liked the one about men growing large vegetables, and would I like to join them at their next filming session in Birmingham.

Oh! What had I done? Well never mind, I'd go, I could hardly not, after my tirade. It would be fun, but they would see that I was totally unsuitable. Or perhaps I could be rehearsed until I could do something, possibly, though now it seemed doubtful, possibly something nearly as good as Cyril Fletcher. How fear humbles one. I turned up on the appointed day, still in denial. It was really rather fun. I watched the filming. We had lunch at a nice Italian restaurant. Diners turned to stare at us – well I don't think that they were staring at me actually, but fame with no responsibility. I could get used to that.

At the end of the afternoon's filming I felt quite confident. Nobody had said anything to me as to my involvement, nor would they, they had obviously realised that I was so unsuitable that they had not bothered to tell me anything about the programme making process. The producer would shake hands, say, "We'll let you know" and that would be that.

This confidence sprang from the culmination of several discoveries about the 'off the cuff' nature of the programme: that the programme was not scripted in any way, was shot in one take, and as far as I could see was not rehearsed in any way either. Could it have been rehearsed last week? But then where was this week's rehearsal? No it seemed indeed to be just made up as they went along. There was no way that I could do that. I wasn't a professional, I whined to myself. They couldn't expect me to. Surely it would be obvious – of course it would – conveniently forgetting that I was there at my own suggestion.

"O.K." the producer said, "See you in two weeks time, and could you bring some large vegetables?"

What? Oh be careful what you wish for! No advice as to what exactly I was expected to do. No, "Rehearsals will be on Tuesday afternoon and Wednesday morning." Just – see you next time.

I spent the next two weeks in a haze of fear. I scoured the area for obscenely large vegetables; they were not to be found – just rather large ones – looking nothing at all to get worked up about. I suppose all the huge ones were in shows being lovingly polished by their proud male owners. I worried, ridiculously, about what I was going to wear. Suit and high heels? Not that I had a suit and high heels. Dungarees and wellies? No – too much. I settled on trousers (decent) shirt (ditto), and light sweater. But what if it was very cold and I was blue and shivering, and everyone else was in heavy coats? What if it rained – would that sweater go with my waterproof jacket? Could I hold a pumpkin and an umbrella? Ridiculous now, and actually … ridiculous then, but there were no female garden presenters for guidance. Fanny Craddock sometimes cooked in full evening dress without even a pinnie. Oh my! Evening dress perhaps! – Calm down – no.

On the day – husband and children, no way they were going to miss this (besides I needed a driver didn't I?) were banished to the far end of the park.

"Look I'm nervous enough O.K? Just don't come anywhere near me."

Surely, surely, there would be some rehearsal, some discussion of what was to happen. I must have missed it surely. But no.

"Could you stand over there Ruth, with your large vegetables? Cyril and Bob will come and talk to you." That was it.

I was so nervous I could see that I was making other people nervous for me. Like me, I could see in their eyes that they thought that I was going to bomb. Not helped either by Cyril Fletcher muttering,

"I don't know what we are doing this item for. Husbands and wives have just got to discuss what size of vegetables they want." He was soothed with the observation that while he and his wife might be able to communicate on this subject, there were probably lots of less lucky and verbal people out there who couldn't, and who needed our help.

My, looking smaller by the minute, vegetable collection was duly carried down to the appointed spot, having been snatched from me by card carrying union members whose job this was. Nice job too – set up wires etc. in morning – wait around, carrying the odd large vegetables, till the outside broadcasting paraphernalia was cleared away the next day.

I stood trembling at my post. Bob and Cyril sauntered towards me, chatting in a relaxed manner. They stopped in front of me.

"Now, here we have Ruth Jennings," began Cyril Fletcher, "she has written in complaining that we men (we men indeed!), that we men grow our vegetables far too large – so let's hear all her complaints."

All my complaints! I don't know if I would have burst into life if I hadn't been so outraged, but anyway, suddenly I was totally relaxed.

" I think you're making me sound much worse than I actually am." I managed.

Cyril was slightly taken aback. The discussion progressed, I have no idea what was said, but – one take – it was all over.

People rushed down from the outside broadcast vans to tell me how great I had been, even Cyril and Bob congratulated me. I'm not sure whether this was all a huge rush of relief that I'd managed to utter anything at all, and hadn't cried or fainted, but everyone seemed very pleased with me. I got a nice letter from the producer and a commemorative photo. When I watched the show, together with the half dozen or so children brought in for the occasion by my own, I looked totally relaxed and at ease ... a pattern was forming.

I really think that I could have done this some more if I had pushed it. Later on someone who appeared far more amateurish than me took over – but I found it far too scary. Thinking about it now, I had actually got the scary bit over. It probably would have seemed easier from then on.

I hope that I won't dispel TV's magic for anyone if I reveal that two weeks broadcasts were actually filmed at the same time, so another programme was filmed in the afternoon.

Theme of the following week's programme? How to grow giant vegetables.

My TV appearance was not my only dalliance with the media at this time. Nor the only occasion on which I volunteered myself for something while not in possession of any of the relevant facts, and then discovered them too late.

I was beginning to try my hand at writing. Perhaps if I didn't have to decide what to wear it would be easier. You don't have to decide what to wear on the radio do you? Well I suppose you do, but it's not exactly a matter of life and death is it? I suppose few people would consider it a matter of life and death at other times – but you know what I mean.

We had been having a bit of trouble with our piano. It had been purchased originally, at great expense, to grace the front room of my in-laws house. No-one could play it, and after the said initial expense there was probably no money left over for piano lessons. Piano lessons? Why? Isn't it enough to have your front room enhanced by a nice large piano? Unfortunately it had attracted the attention of my husband's younger brother, who, presumably at a loss as to what to do with it, decided to give it a good 'seeing to' with a brick. What the brick was doing in the front room is open to speculation.

Anyway, as my husband was the only one with even aspirations to play the piano, we had inherited it. It joined us in our bungalow, sharing our new baby's tiny room. Perhaps its presence would make him musical – new parents think like this. Besides we had nowhere else to put it.

Years later bumping into our removal men, they still remembered how extraordinarily heavy our piano had been. They hadn't worded it quite like that.

It accompanied us to our second home, where in an attempt to banish its tattiness to an upstairs room – to be known as the 'music room' it nearly demolished the banisters of our brand new house. These (different) removal men, also now no doubt with memories to treasure, insisted that it stayed downstairs.

In our third house, piano still in tow, we decided that we were now far too far up the social scale to support a brick scratched piano, and decided to get it re French polished. That's when we discovered that the front was actually fashioned from a front door

– it even had a keyhole, and was of an entirely different 'front door' type wood. The inside as well was a bit of a mystery, with heavy assorted ironwork that looked as if it too, had been something else originally, possibly an organ, or ... gate. We were attached to it, because when it was in tune, which admittedly wasn't often, it had the most beautiful tone. The Rentokil man had spent a dreamy couple of hours enjoying this beauty, although he was supposed to be enjoying the lesser beauty of our fly cemetery loft at the time.

French polishing ruled out, we then made various attempts to paint it ... spray it ... the story was a long one, involving trying to get it outside using a rolling pin ... impossible ... groin strain ... covering the room in aluminium foil ... plastic sheeting ...

I wrote a piece called – *Our Piano Is Not Our Forte*.

Who would be interested in such a piece? Ignoring the obvious answer that screams at you – nobody – I consulted my *Writers' and Artists' Year Book* and decided on, 'Woman's Hour'.

Amazingly, they *were* interested! Hallelujah – I was a writer!

I was invited to the Birmingham studios at Pebble Mill, for a voice test. A voice test? Why? Actors read these things, didn't they? Or professional readers, I was a writer, not a reader – I couldn't do it. My verdict was not based this time on just unsubstantiated panic. My voice did not record well. It did not record as the voice of a female human person.

The first time I heard my recorded voice was whilst at college. A discussion had been taped. When it was played back I remember thinking "Who is that man?" And then – "Why is he saying what I said?" And then – "This is an all-girl's college." And then – "Oh my God – its me!"

I have been reassured that in real life my voice doesn't sound like that of a man. Even my husband who with diligence, nay enthusiasm, takes it upon himself to make sure that I am aware of my every fault and weakness – even he says that I don't sound like a man. Perhaps it's because faced with, obviously a woman, you don't. I don't know. But recorded I know my voice does not sound right. I feel quite sorry for strangers talking to me on the phone. At the end of a long conversation they will say:

"So could I have your address Mr Jennings?" If I try to save their embarrassment by going along with this, invariably their next question will be, "... and your first name?" If I say, "... well it's Mrs Jennings actually," they are not surprisingly covered in confusion and embarrassment. It is the norm not the exception, so not unnaturally I think, I am a little touchy about my voice.

So here I was being invited for a voice test – well they'd see, wouldn't they? Or rather they'd hear. Either they would need to make some announcement to say please don't phone in, they hadn't got my name wrong. Neither should listeners adjust their radios, or take them back to the shop and complain. Perhaps R. Jennings would cover it. Anyway that was their problem, although they didn't know it yet.

I duly turned up for the voice test, to be told that it wasn't really a voice test at all. If everything was OK – we would record the piece. I sat alone in the middle of the recording studio, trying not to rustle papers. Was it worth trying to speak in a higher octave, I thought? No, too risky, what if I couldn't keep it up and ended up squeaking? Or lost my voice with only the last sentence to go, so that listeners thought that my voice was breaking and that I was an adolescent youth?

To my astonishment the sound engineer came in and said – that was fine, and we would record now. Well I assumed he was a sound engineer – perhaps he was the next, Woman's Hour speaker, on the subject of hearing loss, and what to do about it. A man anyway, came in and said, that was fine, and we would record now.

A pattern then developed – I read a page – my mysterious attendant came in, drew some red lines over part of what I had read, and said,

"Let's try that again, missing out that bit."

This happened to every page. The whole thing stopped making sense, I could see it. I was referring on page four to things that had been crossed off on page two. How was this ever going to work?

Well they must know what they were doing, mustn't they?

Finally we were finished. My new friend – perhaps he was just someone who had wandered in from the street – seemed happy. We shook hands. I would hear from Woman's Hour in the near future he said. I went home and waited. After a couple of weeks I enquired as to how things were going.

"Oh you'll hear very soon now." A few weeks later, the same exchange. After another attempt I gave up and forgot all about the whole thing.

A year later I received a polite little note from Woman's Hour saying that they were sorry but that they couldn't use my contribution.

Chapter Eight

I was getting very interested in writing now. I had given myself a year off from teaching to see if I could earn a living from writing. I couldn't, but the year stretched into forever. Past experience had shown that I didn't want to be seen – I didn't want to be heard – I wanted to achieve acclaim facelessly, mutely, no clothing decisions to be made. What could I do?

What I really wanted to do was to write for children – how hard could that be? It was for children for goodness sake! The curse of Barnet had not left me – it was alive and well. I wrote lots and lots of children's stories. I enjoyed writing them, and I thought they were good. I posted them off to publishers and got a lot of rejection slips and some encouraging remarks in return, but no acceptances. Then one day, rather like Woman's Hour in reverse, I got a letter saying,

"The story that you sent us a year ago – we love it and would like to publish it – so sorry, we seem to have forgotten to tell you."

My joy was unconfined. This was what I had wanted to do all along. I had found my perfect job! They were even offering me £100 advance … an advance … me … and, a whole £100.

Actually my joy was not totally unconfined. There was a tiny worm of worry wiggling about at the back of my mind. This was not at all a story that I had expected to be chosen. It was a bit of an, 'amusing myself' make-weight, included once in an offering to a publisher along with what I thought were my more commercial offerings. It actually featured my recognisable husband and named sons, and not in a good light, variously: lazy, whining, unreasonable, incompetent, and ultimately it ended in disaster.

The story was called, *In the Bin*. A problem immediately, given the desirability of international sales. *In the Trash Can* or *In the Garbage* did not have at all the same ring. But the publishers did not seem put out by this. The story basically – taken from life – was of two untidy, messy, boys, one a lazy dawdler, and the other prone to ... I wanted to say 'whingeing' but I didn't know how to spell it and couldn't find it in the dictionary, so I put 'wailing' instead. I was usually meticulous about detail but hey! What did it matter? No-one was interested in what I wrote anyway. That 'wailing' was to be surprisingly annoying. Their father, again taken from life, was always saying to them:

"If you don't pick these toys up off the floor – I will throw them all in the bin."

So far this was not fiction – it was gritty reality. But then I mused – what if the boys whinged and dawdled themselves to sleep among the toys, and father ... mm ... he was going to have to be a bit short-sighted, and where was mother? She would have to be out. But what if he gathered up the boys with the toys and actually threw them all in the bin.

That was the gist of it. How were the family going to respond? Was I going to have to choose between fame, and being ostracised by my loved ones? My husband said that he didn't mind how I portrayed him as long as I made a lot of money and he could retire and live a life of wanton luxury, at my expense. The boys, well they were young enough to be hoodwinked. How could I have guessed that in the future one would quote from it in his best man's speech at his brother's wedding? Needless to say his own role in the story was somewhat glossed over.

This was really exciting stuff. I'd done my bit now I could just sit back and enjoy. As always it wasn't quite so simple. It was a story for small children, it needed illustrations. I had done very well at art at school by dint of always keeping my border neat and the correct width, and the art teacher liking me. I couldn't help noticing that a girl who really was good at art but who refused to bother with a border, and whom the art teacher did not like, got substantially lower marks than me. My success with neat borders did not unfortunately enable me to illustrate my book.

The publisher had an illustrator in mind. I saw examples of his previous work. It was brilliant – just right, layer upon layer of detail – I loved it. Then amazingly, I discovered that he lived nearby. Could I, dare I, contact him? I phoned. He sounded friendly, normal. Why do we always suppose that people who 'do' things are a different species to us? I went to see him. To be honest he was a bit out of the ordinary, but then he was an artist. Trouble was, like a lot of people who are very good at one thing, he really hankered to be good at something else. He spent long periods following up other ideas – delving into games based on the periodic table, studying obscure subjects, reading weighty, time-consuming tomes on every subject under the sun. What he did not spend a lot of time doing was illustrating. I liked him, I wished him well, I admired his talent, but most of all, this was my big chance, I willed him not to let me down.

Eventually the illustrations were done. They weren't his most elaborate, but they were good. There was some fine-tuning of the words to be done too. A stream of small requests arrived. Could I change this bit here, re-word that bit there? Shades of the piano piece began to surface. By the time I had made all the small alterations there was scarcely a sentence untouched, and although the story was the same, it didn't have quite the same rhythm. To be honest, I wasn't crazy about it, but I supposed that all great writers suffered this indignity and had to bear it.

They did want me to change the ending too, but I held firm here. Dustmen return sleepy boys to horrified father – boys returned to bed, don't remember incident at all – remain untidy. Traumatised father never forgets, or says ever again: "If you don't pick up these toys…"

Couldn't I be a bit kinder to father? No. Couldn't the boys be a bit tidier? No. At the end of the day – it was my story. Was this 'artistic temperament?'… ooo … I must be a real artist now.

The book was published. This was news in my neck of the woods; I was photographed for the local paper with my book, and a group of suitably impressed looking children. I never did get to do any book signing sessions though, but I did make it to a publisher's party. After the inevitable 'what to wear crisis' (cat suit and heels? cat haired cardigan and slippers? dirndl skirt and sandals?) I quite enjoyed it. Shit-scared I've been, traumatised I've been, but shy I've never been.

"Scary isn't it?" I said comfortingly to one miserable looking man skulking in a corner. "Is this your first time too?"

"No," he said, followed by silence.

"Oh ... " I gave up, and wandered off to try my comforting on some other poor soul.

He turned out to be a very famous children's author who had probably been to more publishers' parties than I had had hot dinners. How was I to know? Children's authors then were not recognisable celebrities.

The book sold well at first, then sales kind of tailed off. I don't know how many copies children's books normally sell, but suffice to say, it did not become a best seller. What excuses can I make? Perhaps I am kidding myself, but it was a bit unfortunate. Its release coincided with two other factors – a sudden huge hike in the price of children's picture books – it seemed very expensive. What caused this sudden plate shift, I don't know, but although it got very good reviews (in the national press, no less) the fact that it was very expensive for what it was, was mentioned several times. Did this mean that that I was a greedy author making a fortune? Well no. The price decided on had nothing to do with me, and I got 4p per copy in royalties.

The other unfortunate thing was that another illustrated children's book came out at exactly the same time, and although it was the same price, it had the added attraction of containing clues to a treasure hunt for a real and valuable prize. This got an enormous amount of publicity.

Enough of excuses – what happened to my precious first born

book? The royalty cheques were clearly never going to support that luxury life style. They ended up as a source of rueful amusement ... £1-20p ... 24p ... 16p ... and then it was remaindered.

But never mind I had done it once, I could do it again. After all, I had those all-important contacts now, and I was a published author. However, try as I may, I couldn't do it again. Why is it only occurring to me now, that I was the published author of a book that had not done terribly well, it might even have represented a loss to the publishers. Hardly the career boost that I saw it to be. However, I got lots of encouraging responses to further offerings – this story would be kept in mind for an anthology... that never quite made it. That story was great if they could just find an illustrator ... then ... illustrators didn't want to take it on – it was going to be too difficult. Illustrators on the whole like to illustrate their own books.

A comment made a couple of times was that I wasn't really, truly, writing for children. I was really writing for adults. Adults I supposed with my silly and rather black sense of humour ... mmm ... perhaps they had a point. This wasn't necessarily unsuitable for children, they liked 'silly'... and black humour, but given my two other best friends, irony and sarcasm ... yes perhaps they did have a point. Perhaps I should be writing for adults.

Chapter Nine

So – I would write a book for adults. That was decided then.

I had always had the idea that you could write any way that you wanted to. Obviously you couldn't write about quantum physics, or care home management if you didn't know anything about them and couldn't be bothered to research. But for less specialised topics, surely it was just up to you. Style seemed even more open to personal choice: heavy, light, acerbic, witty – these would clearly be a matter of choice.

I knew what I wanted to do. I wanted to write something serious, intellectual and dense with meanings ... a masterpiece, no less. Something which would be worthy of discussion at the 'Workers' Education Association' (WEA) literature class that I attended. The 'workers' of the title, incidentally, are debarred from this class by dint of it being on a Tuesday morning, when they are all at work. It was, and is, made up of a group of scarily clever women, who between them appear to have read every book ever written. They can cross reference with ease chapter four of Faulkner's *The Sound and the Fury* with chapter eight of *War and Peace* and spot a 'stream of consciousness' from several streets away. I have read whole shelves of books and been totally unaware that they were 'stream of consciousness' or 'magic realism'. I was always saying things like – "Didn't he cross the road to get to the other side?" Shock, horror – of course he didn't – he is crossing the forbidden boundary to enlightenment. I don't say too much these days. I try to keep my thoughts to myself. Glad I didn't suggest that the significance of Proust eating that madeleine was to show that he was a bit peckish, nor that he dipped it in his tea just because it probably seemed a bit stale. Seemed it was all about something entirely different.

Why do I subject myself to this humiliation? Because, while the others attend because they love to read, I go because otherwise I might never read any 'worthwhile' books, if I didn't have to do it for next Tuesday. Just wish I could get this *Ulysses* even opened before next Tuesday.

One compliment however that was paid to me at this class I have treasured ever since. My neighbour turned to me and said,

"I do so admire you."

"Really?" ... I waited for some pretty compliment about my wit, or perceptive contributions.

"Yes ... you seem to be able to wear so few clothes."

I looked down at my tee shirt, and cotton cargo pants – so becoming to women in their sixties, I always think. I looked around – true – everyone else was wearing woolly jumpers, some even jackets. Perhaps I was the only one who felt the intellectual heat – but my only admirable quality? Oh dear! However it is almost a pleasure to be humiliated by this international collection of intelligent and lively women.

Perhaps there is another reason why I persevere, one that in truth I'd rather forget. My mother belonged to a WEA literature group in the '40s and '50s. The WEA was really aimed at people like her; a working woman who had missed out on education, and wanted to improve herself. The poor woman got home from the shop after six o'clock, had a meal to cook, and then out to her class – by public transport, remember. When she had time to read the books I can't imagine. When I asked her what had happened at her ... sniff ... poncey ... class, she had often fallen asleep, or had not had time to finish the book. I'm afraid I was scathing about what I saw as her pretentious attempt to be someone she was not. Heavens, she even read the Sunday Times – who did she think she was? Ah that reminds me – the paper bill – isn't the Sunday Times expensive these days?

65

I have now had many years of sitting in the same class, often with my bookmark at page thirty five, and occasionally drooping eyelids, to ponder on my casual teenage cruelty and the strange circular nature of life. One of my sons, now buying wine by the case, and discussing the relative merits of New Zealand Sauvignon Blancs, as a teenager accused us of only drinking wine to try to appear middle class. More upsetting than the intended jibe, was the implication that we were not already bona fide members of the middle class. He at least came to a rapid, about face, downfall – of the worst sort – the 'before your parents die' downfall. He chose to 'study' viticulture as part of his university course. Field trips to Portugal to 'sample' wines; field trips to France to 'study' champagne, left him literally and metaphorically without a leg to stand on. He was forced to eat his words – with a nice bottle of Beaujolais, of course.

I digress – and not, you may have noticed, for the first time.

I have like most of the others, attended this literature class for many years. I used, in the old days, before the intellectual temperature rose to vaporising point, to write pieces for the annual anthology. Things like, *Mrs Bovary Joins The WEA,* or I'd imagine that we were the preserved group of extinct intellectuals in *The Reservation* sitting stuffed and naked in our circle for future generations to gawp at. Our tutor at that time was a lady of immense character and intellect, and formidable opinions, and I was teacher's pet. She was pretty shameless. No-one wanted to read anything out after me because it would be made clear that it was a ghastly anticlimax. My opinion, however 'off course' was always elicited. Ah ... the good old days. The rest of the class put up with this behaviour with admirable tolerance. The situation was tested to breaking point when she set up a short story writing competition. Her nephew who was a publisher was to be the judge. No-one was in any doubt that this was for my benefit. Imagine her outrage when I came second.

My story was called *The Heroine Addict* and was about a woman who took on the personalities of the heroines in the books she read – a bit of fun for a literature class I thought. My heroine read *Madame Bovary* – she became moody and dissatisfied with her lot. *Gone with the Wind* – she acquired ringlets, a tinkling laugh and took to sharing mint juleps with her next door neighbour, Mr Butler ... then finally ... *The Borgias – The Poisoning Years*. But arriving home from the chemist with the poison, she notices that her somehow darker and more menacing looking husband, is reading – *Othello*.

The winning story was a moving account of a woman in a hospital cancer ward as she awaited her mastectomy, and contemplated her mortality. Mmm ... so similar ... hard for the judge to separate. Bad luck for him I suspect. Certainly the poor winner was treated as if she was an imposter who had deliberately stolen my crown. Was the nephew cut out of his aunt's will I wonder?

Anyway this book that I was going to write was going to be different, serious, heavy; they were going to discuss it and love it. I could picture it now. I wouldn't be there of course, modesty would forbid it. I would be on a lecture tour of America, or a book signing in Australia, or sunning myself in the Bahamas trying to avoid media attention. But the rest of the class would be there with furrowed brows. They would find existentialism in it perhaps, or magic realism. Would I have put them there? Or would they be just, well ... finding them? As I suspected they sometimes did. Perhaps they would discuss my use of the words 'I' or 'well'. Repeated words never appeared in 'good' books merely because they kept popping unbidden into the mind of the writer. Oh dear me no! They always 'meant' something. Did my use of 'I' cleverly mean 'eye' as in the way I saw things? Perhaps my use of 'well' was a reference to my drawing upon my subject matter from the depths of my psyche – from some deep dark place in my mind – a hidden spring of inspiration or pain. Or perhaps I used it to signify man's striving towards a state of being spiritually, 'well' as opposed to the inherent, 'un-wellness' of the human condition.

I was encouraged by these thoughts. I could stop trying not to use 'well' – well it was difficult. I could now class it as symbolism. I would like my writing, like my reading to be full of symbolism, to trap the lazy reader.

Why did Mathieu stab himself in the hand? Because he had gone a bit barmy? No – to show the existential possibilities that we hold over our destinies. Why did Charles climb the Martello tower? To get a better view of *The Sea the Sea*? Of course not. It symbolised him climbing above the physical world to get a better view of life and the mundane, the latter symbolised by the sardines he had every day for his lunch – and no – if you had just thought that he liked sardines you were wrong again. I wanted to write like this. I wanted to be ... so... so ... annoying ... actually.

I wanted to write like Umberto Eco, he was annoying. He said that he deliberately made the first hundred pages of his books really difficult and boring to ensure that only the worthy reader could, 'climb the mountain' as I think he put it. Wouldn't want any old hoi polloi reading your books now would you? It succeeded – my bookmark never got past page thirty. Mmm ... perhaps I wouldn't write *exactly* like Umberto Eco, unless of course my book was only twenty nine pages long, and I wasn't aiming for a slim volume.

I knew clearly how I wanted to write, but the truth was – I couldn't. The whole idea that you could write whatever and however you liked was deeply flawed. In a flash of insight, I saw that I have an odd, and not very serious way of looking at things, and would need surgical assistance to get my tongue out of my cheek, and that's the only way that I can write. Also that in order to plumb the intellectual depths, you need an intellect deeper than the average paddling pool, and while I might stretch to the 'swimmers only beyond this point' at the municipal baths, I was never going to find myself tackling the meaning of life, the human condition, or Greek type tragedy. It was obvious, I saw now; that is how everyone writes – how they see things ... and how they can.

It turned out to be a wee bit academic anyway. Not only could I not write that existentialist, post modernist, stream of conscious, impress your friends type of book – however hard I chewed my biro, however much I paced up and down, I couldn't think of any subject for a book of any kind, not only not heavy, but not even a book that was lightweight, silly or shallow. I comforted myself with the notion that getting a book published, even if I had been able to write one, would have been difficult. I had saved myself a lot of work and frustration. Everyone was writing books. There was really no need for any more.

Why not try something that had a need to be filled? Why not try magazines? I suspect that magazines are now all syndicated, but in those days you were free to send in freelance items. There were dozens, if not hundreds of magazines with pages to fill on a weekly or monthly basis, I reasoned. And a lot of the stuff wasn't very good – silly trivial articles, corny stories, bad writing. I could do better than that.

Lesson learned – do not ever think that anything you read is there because they can't find anything better. It is there because it is exactly what they want. As usual, happy in my ignorance, I set about raising standards in magazine publishing.

I'd try articles. The good thing about articles I realised, is that you could write in advance and say, "Would you be interested in an article on the history of plant pots of "… quick count up of words in said magazine's articles, "… of two thousand words". If they said,

"No thanks," at least it saved you having to write it. On one occasion someone said, 'maybe' and I couldn't think what to write. There is a balance to be struck between wasting your time writing things no-one wants, and suggesting that you will write things, when you either can't, or don't want to. The idea of writing articles fizzled out because I couldn't find much that I knew enough about to write an article, and was basically not willing to put in the research.

No, I was really a fiction writer I reckoned. I'd try romantic short stories. Women's magazines at that time went though masses of them – three, usually to an issue. You couldn't really apply the ... 'would you be interested in ...?' save yourself time approach.

"Would you be interested in a story about a girl who meets a boy; at first they don't like each other, she thinks he's stuck up, when really he's just shy. He thinks she's interested in his friend, because he sees them together, helping a lame puppy, but after a series of other misunderstandings, they finally sort things out and live happily ever after."

Mmm ... hard to tell really. Perhaps if there were a bit more detail. Well then, how about this ...?

Plain, mousey, orphan, goes to work as governess for dark, broody man in gloomy house on moors. Despite her being poor (she's not really as it turns out) and him rich, they fall in love. They can't marry because of mad wife in attic. Mad wife burns down house and herself, and leaves man broodier than ever and blind, but eventually mousey orphan and broody man marry and live happily ever after in sunny, cheery house in South of France.

Mmm ... I'm afraid I think it would still elicit the same sort of response.

"Dear Ms Bronte, thank you for sending us the synopsis of your story, *Jane Eyre,* unfortunately we do not think it will fit our current list requirements. PS. Please send stamped addressed envelope and return postage if sending us further ideas."

No ... you had to actually write them first.

I managed to keep my tongue out of my cheek – not a good place for it to be when writing romantic fiction – for long enough to sell a few stories to *My Weekly* magazine. I received the grand sum of £15 for the first, and no, it wasn't a lot even then. It had taken me a week to write it, and it was one of several that had each taken me a week to write but that I had not sold.

I reckoned I was earning £2-50 for a seventy hour week. I mention this for anyone who assumes that all writers are regularly flying off to New York in order to shop on 5th Avenue, on the backs of their vast earnings. Still, I told myself, everyone has to start somewhere. I finally gave up knocking on this particular door when the, I thought, clever, pithy, and altogether brilliant ending that I had used for one story was changed to … 'and so they had a nice cup of tea'.

Pleeeaaase!

Given this modest success with romantic fiction, I wrote the first couple of chapters of a Mills and Boon type romantic novel, and sent them off to a publisher.

"Yes please," they said. "We'd like to see the rest." Trouble was that I hadn't written the rest, and I really didn't want to write it. I'm not knocking romantic fiction writing, it's exactly as difficult as any other sort of writing, but my heart just wasn't in it.

She magazine was more my style. They didn't want romances at all. They accepted my story about the Union Jack chamber pot, and the one about the man who took the notice on his park lake saying, 'Rowing boat hire – as long as you like – 75p' literally, and spent his summer holidays in a rowing boat, with subsequent media attention. I thought it would make a good radio play (safe in the knowledge that I wouldn't be expected to play all the parts) but the BBC drama department didn't agree. Then, at the time of a court case where the judge had decreed that a young woman had contributed to her rape by her choice of clothes, I sent my main character walking through Coventry late at night in a boob tube and hot pants, to exercise her rights.

It was while I was writing for *She* that the competition came up. *She* was running a short story competition, and the rules did not debar me – well of course, I'd have a go. There was one major problem – the subject. It had to be a crime story and I didn't do crime, not literally, not literarily. Again, I racked my brains and chewed my biro. I could think of not one idea for a short story, a long story, a paragraph even on the subject of crime.

A murder? train robbery? gangsters? forgery? gritty policeman … Brahms loving detective? Oh dear, crime was just so not me. Despite hundreds if not thousands of authors making a living out of writing crime fiction year in year out, not even one idea could I produce. In desperation and still with a totally blank mind, I tried sitting down and just writing an opening sentence, any old opening sentence, just ... anything.

'The old man limped across the street ... he saw ...' what? Fizzle out.

'She pressed herself against the wall, hiding behind the potted plant ... and ...?'

'The car screeched to a halt and the ... six foot gangster? ... four foot midget? got out ... he looked puzzled?... angry?... happy? ...' yes ... so? Nothing.

And then I wrote – 'Always late is Gary' ... and a whole story just wrote itself. It took about an hour, pretty well word perfect. I looked at it in amazement. I liked it. Who wrote that? Was it me?

I proceed here with caution. Probably better not to proceed at all – but hey! Reckless disclosures are so me. I just seemed to pull on a few short threads, and then one that just kept coming. Coming from where? I'm more than a bit embarrassed here, because what am I talking about ... 'inspiration?' 'Heavenly intervention?' This may or may not have happened to Shakespeare, Wordsworth, Dostoevsky, but hold on, this was a short story for *She* magazine, hardly likely to attract the attention of the muses. Funny though, how so many writers describe this same – 'where did that come from?' feeling. There is probably some perfectly logical and scientific explanation, like electrical brain activity misfiring when you die, perhaps causing you to see bright lights. Perhaps with sustained brain activity – even futile brain activity, all your synaps line up, and ideas flow through better. I am a fully paid up member of the sceptics society, but could we know everything there is to know? Recently my husband pouring himself a coffee into an un-cracked, un-chipped, mug was amazed to see it split from top to bottom and the coffee pour out. A couple of hours later we got a phone call to say that the friend who had given us that mug had died at exactly that time. Coincidence doesn't quite seem to cover it.

And it is kind of scary looking at a piece of writing, however humble, and thinking, 'did I do that? How?' Perhaps it's just called

– having a good day. Certainly, having a bad day, is a well known and accepted concept.

It couldn't have been top grade, triple milled inspiration anyway, because I came second – again. But I was well pleased with my second place – glory, publication – and my winnings. Three figures no less, a typewriter … and a writing course, with one of those outfits that advertise, 'Why not be a Writer?' Why not indeed? 'Take our course and you could be the next Dan Brown, or J K Rowling, and be fighting publishers off with a stick.'

This was obviously 'meant'. I would complete this course, using my brand new typewriter, and sustained with chocolate éclairs, Brazilian coffee, and the odd glass of superior wine – bought with my winnings. Right – what did I need to do?

'Before we begin, just fill in this box telling us a bit about yourself.'

Could I do that? I could not. On and off for weeks I tried to tell them a bit about myself. Which bits would they want to know? How to write it? Somehow I just couldn't get it quite right. Why I thought it so important to impress someone with my writing, before, I began the writing course, I can't now get my head round. But as weeks turned into months, and every time I told myself to get on with it, I found myself cleaning the oven, or going for a long walk, I realised that all the tutors would have gone on to write their own best sellers. Nobody would be left at the writing school who would know anything about me, or my prize. I realised I had wasted my chance. I would never write *Bridget Jones' Diary* now, or *Harry Potter and the Goblet of Fire*, I had blown it.

The story? Oh, it was called, *Mr Big*. It was about a gang of boys hanging around in a city centre. They decide to break into an electrical shop and help themselves to some expensive equipment. They study the row of shops from the front – OK it's third from the left. They go round to the back and count third from the left, and end up breaking into a Chinese take-away, and stealing a frozen duck. So? OK, it was a frozen duck … It wasn't much of a crime I grant you … but it was still a crime.

Chapter Ten

I liked writing for *She*, but even here I was still spending a lot of time writing things that weren't published. Writing is different to other areas of creative endeavour. If you paint a picture and no-one else likes it, you can put it up on your own wall and admire it yourself. You can put flowers in your only slightly lop sided pottery vase, wear your own, rather chunkier than intended jewellery, but unpublished writing is just a pile of paper in a drawer, and the realisation that your children are going to dump it. I was working a lot and only succeeding a little. My drawer was full, I needed something more concrete. How about writing for a local newspaper? They wouldn't have the luxury of time to reject my offerings.

I have always loved local newspapers. I find them a wonderful source of the kind of humour that really appeals to me. The humour was always unintentional, but all the better for that. Not that I would be contributing to the humour, I hoped.

When we moved to this area, I scoured the local papers for clues as to where would be a good place to settle. Front page of our local paper on that occasion was a heated, angry, hound them out of town type attack. Somebody had put a small thatched porch over the door of their cottage, and it was of quite, but quite, the wrong period. How could they be so wicked? Wow! If this was the worst thing that happened around here – this was the place for me.

This same paper has given me countless hours of joy over the years. Its editor when we first arrived was a familiar figure cycling round the town in search of the latest 'hot' story. Who could resist the item about the lady who went to her W.I. meeting, inadvertently leaving her car lights on, and came out to find her battery flat? Or the one headed – 'Nice One Squirrel'('Nice one Cyril' being a popular saying of the time) about someone seeing a squirrel up a tree and wondering if it was in trouble, but passing later noticed that it had disappeared and so assumed that it was alright.

Honest – I am not making these up – well you couldn't make them up, could you?

More recently, I felt quite sorry for the man who, objecting to flats being built overlooking his garden, said that he was a naturist, and that his rights to nudity in his own garden would be compromised. An enterprising reporter not only got an interview with him, but managed to persuade him to pose, in the nude, with only a mower to cover his vital bits; fascinating enough, but what was really interesting was, that while his arms legs and face were nut brown, the rest of him was surprisingly pale; he must have spent a lot of his time as a naturist, sitting in the shade.

No wonder when a reporter – tipped off by a 'friend' – came to interview me on my wildly important TV appearance on 'Gardening Today,' I was not happy. Indeed I became so unhappy that she said, with enormous charity and kindness:

"Would you like me to say that you weren't in, and tear this up?"

"Yes … yes … please" I choked. I have visions of having hugged her in grateful relief.

She had started asking questions about whether my husband was interested in gardening. He isn't – not in the slightest. He is proud of the fact that he would not be able to tell the difference between a dahlia and a delphinium. I was very nervous. Could I check the copy? No, sorry. The headline? Sorry, the editor took it upon himself to write the headlines.

I had visions of:

'Husband In Pub As Gardener Plants Tub,' or –

'TV Gardener Says That Husband Is A Lazy Bastard.' Well no,

not quite – we have no swearing in our local paper ... oooo; imagine the fuss that that would cause.

But my heart and all my sympathy, goes out to the reporter who one week reported that a sick local councillor had died. The councillor had not died. The following week there was an abject, hand wringing apology for the mistake ... distress to the family etc. Followed the following week by the announcement that said councillor had really died now ... no ... really ... it's true this time.

How difficult could being a writer on a local paper be? I would answer the advertisement for a copy-writer on the sister publication. If I made mistakes – heck – who would notice?

As ever, things were not as simple or straightforward as they seemed. Why did mistakes slip through? Because you had an enormous amount to do, and very little time to do it in – as I soon discovered.

My job was to write the property and advertising copy.

What the former turned out to mean was that every week I was to choose a dozen houses from the estate agents' advertisement pages, and write about them.

But ... someone had already written about them – the estate agent. I had no other information. Hadn't the estate agent's blurb already said: 'cul-de-sac, 3 bed, large bath, gardens front and rear?' Yes, but I had to do it the same ... but somehow different ... i.e:

'This beautiful property standing in a prime position in a quiet (hope this was true) cul-de-sac, boasts three lovely bedrooms, and benefits from a spacious bathroom. It has the added advantage of having gardens, with things growing in them, to the front of the property ... and to the rear.'

You get the idea. Doing twelve of these, week in and week out, and trying to make them sound different, and interesting was a challenge. Wow, three bedrooms! ... not a ... downstairs cloakroom!... A garden? Really?...You're kidding me?!'

There was also a weekly 'Star Property'. This was a featured house with even more written 'wow' factor. It didn't have to have much 'starry' about it, just come within quite a tight price band,

and I had to go and interview the vendors, so that I could write things like –

'Mr and Mrs Hardcastle have lived in their beautiful home for five years and just love their proximity to the railway line that runs along the bottom of their garden, as they are very interested in trains, and like to record the sounds of the various train noises – night time usage of train whistles is their special interest. No come to think of it, perhaps not a good idea. What about –

'Mr and Mrs Hardcastle just love their avocado bathroom suite, and will find it hard to tear themselves away from it, but they are relocating to Spain where they hope to find one exactly like it.'

This feature was, for some reason, particularly hard to do. I had to see someone at the weekend to get copy in on time. The property needed to have some potential to say something interesting, and the price band was a further restriction. People were strange too. One couple let me come and see them, interview them for half an hour, and then the wife said to the husband,

"Haven't we appeared in this feature before?"

"Yes," he said going over to a drawer and producing a cutting of the last time they had appeared as 'Star Property' – a week before I started the job.

I had a problem too, that seems laughable now – how quickly things change. I had interviewed a couple about their flat, then I realised that they had different names. Shock, horror, they were not married. What was I to do? Living in sin, it was still called then – how could I avoid dragging my august paper, and these poor wretches through the mire, and also avoid having to find another star property. I managed a discreet, 'John and Jean are reluctantly leaving their fascinating apartment conveniently situated on the fifth floor…'

Headlines too, continued to throw up problems. They were dreamed up by somebody else, and tended towards the bizarre. I tried making my own suggestions, but however good I thought they were, they were always changed. Nor could I offer any guarantees to nervous interviewees who had also noticed this tendency. One of the worst examples unfortunately concerned someone that I knew from some other job. She let me come and see the house, and I noticed a couple of nice trees in the garden which I commented on in my piece. The feature appeared with the heading:

'Tree Fanatic's House For Sale.'

I wasn't sure whether to phone and apologise, or if that would make it worse. I never heard from her again.

But undoubtedly my biggest, 'Barnet' moment, was an encounter that still ... well, 'haunts' is too strong a word ... still makes me laugh to be honest, was the following:

My technique for dealing with 'Star Properties,' was to phone, introduce myself, ask if they were familiar with my paper, and also, if they were familiar with its 'Star Property' feature. On this occasion there was a long pause after this initial introduction, and then the assurance that my contact was indeed familiar with the paper, and with the Star Property feature, and was indeed even familiar with me – it was my boss, the editor. How could I not have recognised his name? Why had it not caused even the smallest flicker of caution? I stumbled on, trying, and failing, to keep my panic to myself.

"Would you like to come and interview me?" he asked.

"Oh ... er ... no ... it'll be alright on the phone." We were supposed to go and interview in person, and I always, but always, did. I had never conducted this interview on the phone before. How could this be happening to me? I muddled through a few more questions, and then attempted to wind up, and put myself out of my misery – final questions:

"... Where are you moving to?" He told me – hey, what a coincidence – that was my town.

"... and why are you moving there?" There was another long pause.

"Because ... I am about to become editor of the local paper there."

Of course he was! I knew it! Damn, damn, damn!

This is why I could smile with understanding on the three, fourteen year old girls interviewing me in the town centre – I'd been there, done that.

The other part of my job was to write advertising copy. This consisted of writing that little piece about gardening, or Valentine's Day, or Christmas, so that advertisers could have their advertisements for plants, cards, chocolates, grouped round it.

My first piece was a spring gardening one. Now this was something that I knew something about, surely my expertise would be spotted and I would be given a regular column. I had actually written in to this paper offering a weekly, 'Timely Gardening Tips' feature. They had shown zilch interest. Now here they were asking me to write this with no idea or interest in whether I knew anything about the subject or not. I had learned something else about journalism; it's a job and you are expected to just get it done. How you write about something that you know nothing about, is your problem – you don't whinge – you get on with it.

Anyway I did know something about gardening. I called my piece, with great originality, I thought – 'Spring into Summer', before I noticed that everyone calls similarly dated items on almost everything – furniture, cooking, travel, shoes – 'Spring into Summer.' Did they all copy me? Or am I just not very observant? My brilliant gardening item appeared. Nobody said, 'well done', or, 'great piece'. So I learned to just get on with it, it wasn't rocket science, and there was no Nobel Literature prize at the end of it. However, one 'Barnet' moment wasn't enough for me in this job – I managed a second.

This time it was over 'Mother's Day'. Simple enough; write a bit about Mother's Day, to be surrounded by ads for cards, pot plants, and ornaments of little girls holding their dresses out and looking cute.

"Have you forgotten that March 19th is Mother's Day?" I chided, "Shame on you!" I went on to pretty well demolish anyone who could forget this very important date, and the opportunity it presented to buy your mother, chocolates, flowers, or that picture of the crying child that she had always wanted. I was discussing the general wittiness of my piece over dinner one evening when it was pointed out to me that Mother's Day was actually not the 19th of March, but the following Sunday, the 26th of March. I phoned the paper in a panic. Please, please, could someone correct my mistake? I was usually asked to write for the week following, and this had been two weeks away, I burbled.

"I didn't look ... I didn't think."

"Sorry," was the answer, "the paper's gone to bed."

I spent a miserable couple of days watching my career in journalism slip away. But on Friday – heavens be praised, someone, how, I don't know, I wasn't aware that anything was checked in the white heat of local paperdom; someone had spotted my mistake. Mothers everywhere could rejoice – they would get their primulas on the right day after all. And no-one need know about my misplaced moral outrage.

How did this job end? Well, I decided that I was not being paid enough for the amount of work that I was putting in. After all, it wasn't all mistakes, most of it was OK. Some of it was even good. I phoned the editor up, and shared my views with him.

"Well actually," he said, "we really need someone full time now, so thanks for your work, and goodbye."

At least I always seemed to see the funny side, as I put the phone down after speaking to that guy.

Chapter Eleven

Although I could feel my writing juices drying up from a gushing well-spring, to a trickle, to a damp patch, I did surprisingly, manage to squeeze two more jobs out of them before they became the Atacama desert of writing aspirations. My enormous fame as a writer seemed to be spreading. It seemed that it had spread as far as the WEA area organiser. I've got a pretty good idea who spread it in that direction – my, unwavering in her belief in me, WEA tutor, Sue Roseveare. She once asked me what job I was currently doing, listened, and then said,

"Whatever you are doing that isn't writing – you are wasting your time."

That was really sweet of her, though at the time it made me feel bad rather than good, as I had pretty well given up writing at that time. Trouble was – she was alone in this view. None of the recipients of my work shared her rosy view of my talents – not even her publisher nephew, and heaven knows, he must have been leaned upon heavily enough. Could she be right and everyone else in the world wrong? It seemed highly unlikely.

Perhaps I should have borne in mind a similar incident from my past.

In the '50s and early '60s women's lib hadn't reached my neck of the woods, and I was incensed by the unfairness in the way women were both regarded, and treated. I didn't want to just look pretty and keep quiet. And why was it right, that after both working all week, it was my job to catch up with the shopping and housework on Saturday, while my husband spent the day at the rugby club? Or that if I pointed this out I was in danger of being that worst thing a woman could be – a nag. Incidentally I only realised much later that a game of rugby did not last for nine hours.

"So" my husband had said, of my – 'society needs to change' views. "So, I suppose you think that you are right and that everyone else in the world is wrong." Well, I had to admit, that it did seem unlikely. But of course it was soon to be revealed that I was neither wrong nor alone. I'm not blaming him – this was indeed how things seemed at the beginning of the sixties, and he did often cook Sunday dinner while I gardened.

"Against nature," muttered the neighbour who caught us indulging in these clearly unnatural practices. Perhaps I should have given the writing another try.

The WEA area organiser contacted me, and asked if I would be prepared to tutor a creative writing course that they were hoping to run. I drew his attention to the fact that I was a failed writer, and that a successful writer might be a more sensible choice. Obviously desperate, and with considerable ingenuity, he pointed out that a failed writer would be even better to fulfil this post, as I would know how the pupils felt. Did he mean as in not being able to write? Or as in not being successful? Whatever. How could I refuse after that?

The class met one evening a week. They were a mixed bunch, but one alarming thing struck me within a few weeks. Some of them seemed to be able to write as well as I could. Should I be on the opposite side of the table? I sustained myself with my desirability as a failed writer – they hadn't failed yet, had they? So I was still ahead of the field. Looking at this 'logic' now – the 'logic' part of it escapes me.

I organised the sessions to take the form of various exercises: creating characters, plotting, opening paragraphs etc. We would discuss these, then they would write something along those lines at home, bring it the following week, read it out, and we would all discuss their efforts.

The first course went well, my confidence was growing, and I started the second course in the same way. We spent the first evening introducing ourselves, with me asking them all to say what their writing interests were, and what they hoped to achieve. Pretty much same as last time: short stories, articles for magazines, a record for the grandchildren. Then one of the two new guys:

"Romantic fiction."

"OK – fine – there is a good market for romantic fiction in women's magazines."

"Who said anything about women?"

"Er ... OK ... well, let's press on."

His companion's interests were also of the romantic, 'no female involvement' variety.

Like my problem with the unmarried co-habitors, it's almost impossible to imagine now, how such a relatively short time ago, things were so different – but they were. My idea was that whatever the subject set each week, you could apply it to whatever form of writing you were pursuing – wherever your interests lay.

Week 1 – "Julian's eyes met Adrian's in a lingering, smouldering, sex fuelled, stare ... his hands slid down to cradle Adrian's buttocks ..."

Things were grasped, caressed and lingered over. Other things were pushed and pulled. It was done as tastefully as was possible given its content, but total silence greeted the end of these educational revelations – the class was stunned.

"Well," I said brightly, "now what do we think of David's ... er ... beginning?"

Not a word.

"Do you think that he ... um ... captured the mood well?"

Not a word. Not a blink. Not a muscle twitch. They were all terrified of drawing my attention to them, in case I elicited their help. I stumbled on –

"I think he conjured up the feeling of, er ... repressed passion well – would you agree?"

Not a word. I was on my own.

And so it continued every week – more grasping and caressing, joined by throbbing, bulging, and some modest exchanges of bodily fluids. Every week the class left me to struggle on alone. Now although it might still be a bit of a challenge for the tutor, after all, you couldn't prepare – you had a couple of seconds to come up with something to say – not easy. I can't help feeling that perhaps no-one would be that shocked now. It might be no big deal. Perhaps class members would observe in a relaxed manner,

"... Good description of the public toilets there Dave."

"Love the ... night falling over Hampstead Heath ... very ... atmospheric."

Perhaps. But back then this was pushing and grinding against the boundaries – if I can put it like that.

The second job that I came by, in relation to writing, was that of after dinner speaking. It wasn't always preceded by a dinner, but you know what I mean. An acquaintance asked me if I would come and talk to a women's group that she belonged to, about writing. Again I pointed out that I couldn't possibly present myself as a successful writer.

"I could talk about being a failed writer," I joked.

"That's fine," she said, getting out her diary and licking her pencil.

I think that you are supposed to have an agent, but word just kind of spread. Someone from that audience belonged to another group, and so it went on.

I suspect that if you are talking to an audience of men in similar circumstances, a couple of off colour jokes, and a crack about sport, and you are away; but groups of women are quite difficult to second guess. If I told the story about the creative writing class, would they find it funny, or start fidgeting with their handbags? I had the unfortunate belief, that if people weren't actually laughing when I was speaking, they were bored. Sometimes I clicked, but sometimes there was a distressing amount of, 'not laughing'. And the perceived perk of a good meal was reduced to indigestion by the knowledge that I had to speak after it. Perhaps I should have had more wine, or less. Eventually all interlocking women's groups had been exhausted, and the circle closed. I wasn't sorry – I'd been there, done that, what next?

Chapter Twelve

It may seem that the term 'odd jobs' could describe most of what has gone before, but interspersed with them over the years were a whole collection of even odder, even more poorly paid, and even briefer jobs. They are out there, you just have to look for them – and I did. Varied though they were, they mainly come under the heading of 'seemed a good idea at the time'.

The first of them however only answered to 'odd' and 'brief'. I did a short stint covering for an aunt who was running an introduction agency. This was in the '50s when such things were practically unheard of – so it was fascinating stuff. What I remember most vividly, reading through people's descriptions of themselves and their hopes, was the phrase: "I'm looking for someone who will love me for myself." I remember thinking rather callously – well who else would you be loved for? The woman down the road? Marilyn Monroe? I realise now, having a bit more compassion, that this was shorthand for low self esteem, and feeling that if you weren't attractive enough to be loved for your looks, you weren't worthy of being loved at all. You would think that this might be better now, but I fear it is probably worse. Why else would today's women be desperate enough to undergo surgery to improve a nose that no-one else sees as a problem, or liposuction, or face-lifts, unless appearance is even more important now than it was then. Then at least you might have got by on the potential of your child-bearing hips, or your prowess in the kitchen. How did women's lib get us here I wonder?

This next job however, definitely comes under 'seemed a good idea at the time'. I answered an advertisement for home knitters. I liked knitting; I was good at it, and quick. I'd had enough of terrifying myself by going out, wearing suits and facing demons. I would sit at home watching television and knitting, and it was a job too – I would be working, sitting on my sofa, never saying the wrong thing, never getting into scrapes, and earning money – perfect. A lady came round to see me. My first assignment was to knit striped fingerless gloves. She had brought me the pattern, the wool and the needles. She explained that when I phoned to say that I had finished the gloves, she would come back to collect them, pay me, and bring my next assignment. What could be easier, more creative, or satisfying?

Hmmm ... It took me an evening to knit and sew up the first glove, about four hours. That was a long time considering that I was to be paid, as I remember, 50p per pair. I am querying this myself – the 50p I am sure about, but surely it must have been 50p a glove? However if you think about the economics: the lady bringing and collecting has to be paid – two journeys, petrol, travel costs, materials, and someone had to sell them, store costs, profit etc. How much could you get for a pair of fingerless gloves, even hand-knitted? No, I think I am right in remembering it as 50p per pair. That meant that I was earning about 6p an hour. Clearly this was because it was my first glove, I thought; I would get quicker. I might even reach the dizzying heights of a pair an evening and the intoxicating prospect of 12p an hour. But no, I couldn't do it. A striped fingerless glove did take four hours to knit and sew up. I tried to picture women sitting outside their cottages in the Shetland Isles, fingers flying in a blur of supersonic knitting, but still for me it took four hours. It took so much concentration, the finger-stubs, the stripes, the sewing, that I couldn't even watch television either.

I finished my first assignment, and rang my lady. She came round. I pointed out that while I was still willing, I was earning 6p an hour which seemed ... well ... kind of low. She looked around at my comfortable detached home in its half acre garden, patted me on the shoulder and said, "I really don't think this is the job for you dear," and left, taking her patterns, wool, and needles with her.

Another one off job was at a nearby management centre. They had set up a management training exercise and needed some volunteers to be 'managed'. The idea was that over a period of four days they would examine what happened if workers were, or were not, included in management decisions, or told how their work fitted into the bigger picture, and were generally kept in the dark about things. In fact it was designed to prove an already decided premise. Why didn't this surprise me?

It was a lovely job – perfect. No, really, it was, this time. I could cycle or even walk to this establishment – a charming old house set in woodland. We were to get a nice lunch and plentiful supplies of coffee and biscuits were to be provided. And the job? … The job was to fold bits of cardboard at whatever pace I chose. I had no idea why, or what they were for, and I didn't care. Admittedly it might not have been my dream job for life, but for four days it was bliss. No decisions, or responsibility, or stress.

I shared a room with a charming retired man, I would guess in his seventies. He was lovely company. He told me all about his childhood, about the Coventry of his youth, his work, how he met his wife, what had happened to his children. We chatted about this and that, drank coffee, ate biscuits, and folded cardboard. Our mutual happiness and contentment with our situation turned out to be not at all what was required. Because we had no idea about the process before, or indeed what was to happen to our folded cardboard when it left us, we were supposed to be stressed, dissatisfied, and resentful, and have a tiny pile of folded cardboard. Instead we were happy and relaxed and had a huge pile of folded cardboard. Perhaps a lifetime of folding cardboard in ignorance of how our 'cog' fitted into the machine, might have produced a different result, but whose stupid idea was this? And how much money was wasted on it?

I realise that provision of biscuits as an important part of my terms of employment has arisen more than once. Although this shows to my thinking, great restraint, in minimising biscuit references, it might strike an odd note to a reader. For me, biscuits, particularly chocolate biscuits, and custard creams are a significant additional reason for employment outside the home. This being because they do not feature inside the home. The reason for this is that I have precious little (actually – no) self control – would immediately eat them all and be very fat, as opposed to the slightly better option of being a bit overweight. My husband was in the same position, but we felt (pre health police) that it wasn't fair to deprive our children of biscuits. This led to strange conversations in supermarkets.

Me – "Do you like these?" Hold up packet of, as unappetising as possible biscuits.

Husband – "No."

Me – "I don't like them either so ... I'll get them. Do you like these?"

A letter to this effect actually won me a fiver in *Woman* magazine. Even I didn't think this amounted to a career opportunity. As this weakness applies to cakes too, and puddings, and virtually anything with a blob of cream, chocolate etc. clearly my ideal job would be one where the eating of unhealthy food was not only a welcome addition to the job, but also the job itself. Yes, you might be forgiven for thinking that no such job exists ... but you would be wrong.

I don't think it paid well, about £1.50 a session, I seem to remember, and was part time. Obviously the eating of unhealthy food full time, would quite quickly lead to full time sickness, followed by full time death. No – it was a kind of lunch-time job. A kind of, 'Focus Forum for Fatty Food'. A group of us met at the organiser's house to taste food manufacturers' new products, and evaluate them. The problem was that these, 'lunches' represented a far from balanced diet. Sometimes 'lunch' consisted of five types of sausage, two pork pies, a chicken curry, and three flavours of mashed potato. Sometimes even my sweet tooth was challenged, with four chocolate trifles followed by three iced cream cakes, and ice cream. Sometimes there was a suitable mixture, and we could organise it to resemble a meal of sorts: two types of crab paste, three types of pizza, followed by two iced lollies and garlic cheese spread ... mmm ... so difficult to find the right wine, my dear. Sadly for me, but luckily for our health and digestion, we didn't meet very often.

What about competitions? People apparently won more cars than they knew what to do with, and holidays, and BBQs, and even country cottages. This would bypass the notion of me earning money, and move me straight into the acquisition of luxury items. I should be good at it too – the question to answer was usually within the range of my intellectual ability:

"What is 'Kleena' soap powder used for? a) thickening soup b) treating bunions c) washing clothes."

It was the slogan that counted – I could think up good slogans – remember my inspired 'Spring into Summer?' After the purchase of a multitude of products that I didn't want, in order to qualify; I won – nothing – nothing at all. I quickly lowered my expectations from country cottage, car, etc. to ... just ... anything. The competition that finished me off was one that had 500 tea towels as consolation prizes. My brilliant and witty slogan did not even secure one of these. Whatever it took I obviously hadn't got it.

Without even realising it I sometimes drifted into that territory that I said I would never enter – self-employment. I suppose I never noticed because one toe, or even toenail dipped in, followed immediately by failure, caused these minute excursions to not register as employment of any sort.

I noticed in the advertise free 'for sale' columns of the local paper that the price asked for things, varied enormously for similar items. Clearly some people either didn't realise the value of what they were selling, or just wanted to get it out of the way. What if I bought things cheap – did them up a bit – curtains in doll's house windows, lick of paint, etc. and then resold them at a profit? This was way before e Bay of course, and seemed a good idea – well they all did didn't they? After six months the neatly drawn – 'bought' – 'expenses' – 'sold,' columns in my business-like notebook – balanced … just. Not worth it – move on.

Once, when suffering the usual mangetout pea glut and the usual complaints from family (so why do I grow them year after year? Because I can, that's why) I tried a variation on the 'people are starving' line with the 'people would pay a lot' for them line, only to be told – "well sell them then." Yes I know they are supposed to be served in elegant threes and fours, and not half pound piles, but I had masses of the things, and we'd had mangetout soup yesterday, and pureed mangetout the day before. Perhaps tomorrow we would try mangetout and sausage en croute with a rhubarb coulis. Rhubarb was another problem. Rhubarb grew into luxuriant seven foot clumps, and I didn't even like rhubarb. Sustained trawls through recipe books were needed to come up with a slew of recipes using, preferably a lot of rhubarb, but that didn't taste of rhubarb at all. We had once offered dinner guests a choice of three desserts – all rhubarb – I don't think they appreciated our ingenuity. I do hope that wasn't a meal where we served rhubarb sauce with salmon – it might have been. Why did I only seem to be able to grow things that I didn't like, and in huge quantities? Why did I have to cut in half my cherry harvest – one cherry?

So, selling lovely fresh, locally grown produce, why hadn't I thought of it before? I approached one local greengrocer. Mmm, it would be difficult – they couldn't mess their wholesaler about. Yes, I could see that. But the second greengrocer I approached said,

"Yes, OK, bring in what you've got." I brought in my freshly picked mangetout peas. He was pleased. I was pleased to see the start of a satisfying new career – run from home – by bike – hours of guilt-free time in the garden – and my family were delighted.

Then the mangetout peas finished. What now? Well the seven foot rhubarb had by this time flowered, collapsed and existed now only as a pile of stringy, limp, ribbons. So what else was there? Well we had eaten the cherry crop. There was a bit of garlic so tiny that my kitchen staff (husband) refused to use it, a couple of slug endorsed lettuces, and a few stringy beans. I could hardly claim to have mastered continuity of supply. It would be a rash retailer who risked offending his wholesaler on my account. It had been a brief and hopeful flowering as a career, but now it was no more – much better to just give stuff away to friends if you don't want it.

Some ideas quite literally never left the ground. My lawn consisted of 10% grass, 10% weeds, and 80% moss. Hanging baskets were very popular and they were lined with moss, weren't they? Why not rake up all the moss, and sell it to purveyors of hanging baskets. How neat was that? Make a profit out of a problem. However, even to me, the idea of approaching someone and asking – "Could I sell you some moss from my lawn?" seemed daunting. The purveyors of hanging baskets were probably only doing it because their lawns were full of moss too. It wasn't exactly a product in short supply.

I had another horticultural idea – now this really was a good one – honestly. I was good at taking cuttings, and dividing things, and raising plants from seed. This last was aided and abetted by my compost heap, obviously insufficiently heated, it provided a cornucopia of seedlings wherever I used its contents, and not all of them were weeds. A huge estate of new houses was to be built nearby. What if I raised a lot of plants, had some fliers printed, and pushed them through the letterboxes of these new houses – they would all have gardens to fill, wouldn't they? I wouldn't have lots of overheads. I could undercut all those expensive nurseries. Wasn't I constantly shrieking "£6.50 for that? I can't pull them out fast enough – they're weeds in my garden. £4.25 for that – I got a couple of hundred from one packet of seeds."

I set about it with gusto. Dividing, taking cuttings, sowing seeds, lining up rows of pots. Some died. Funny how things can live in the compost heap, or where you don't want them, or re-grow when you have chopped their heads off, but put them in a pot, want them to grow, and suddenly they are prima donnas. Some got eaten by things, or it was too cold, or too hot, or I forgot to water them, or went on holiday, and they were not happy to be left behind. A strange psychology began to take over. I loved my plants, I nursed, cosseted and spoiled them something rotten. (I remember being interrupted once as I was tenderly bedding out some young plants, by the irritating realisation that I would have to break off and put my children to bed.) But these weren't my plants ... quite. They were going to leave me, traitors, I thought illogically. Why should I care? I gradually found that I was losing interest. Have I over intellectualised the problem I had here? Was I just too idle? I think that this was one of my better ideas, not a difficult thing to be, given some of the others, but again it never got off the ground. Did it make me realise the work that goes into raising plants: the pain, the loss, the struggle? Actually, after a brief lull, I returned to saying:

"£5 for that, I throw barrow-loads of those away every week."

So there it was – bad ideas – unable to follow through – obviously, that was why it was a bad idea. But good ideas, also unable to follow through. Self employment, perhaps that was the key – a psyche that had been damaged at an early impressionable age. How could I fight it?

Or was it that I would try *anything* rather than go back to teaching?

Chapter Thirteen

Reaching the age of fifty hit me hard. Twenty, thirty, forty, I had had no problem with, but somehow fifty induced a definite sense of panic. All those things that you promised yourself you would do … one day. One day I'll take singing lessons … one day I'll climb Kilimanjaro … one day I'll go whale watching … one day. Well just how many days did I think I had left, when I would be able to summon up the mental and/or physical ability to do the things that I wanted to do? I felt an urgent need to address whatever I wanted to do – now. While I still could. And I was in no doubt about what I wanted to do – I wanted to travel. Not holiday – travel.

The problem was money. My husband having experienced the sort of travel that I had in mind, did not want to experience it again. On pain of being forced to join me any more in my, I thought, interesting travel exploits he assured me that he was happy for me to go, but just leave him out of it. Going to work, a month of cooking his own meals, coming home to an empty house, all it seemed were preferable to accompanying me on any travel arrangements that I had a hand in. Absenting myself from the matrimonial home was one thing, but raiding the matrimonial piggy bank as well seemed unfair. There was the possibility that he might reap a large insurance cheque given the likelihood of me being trampled to death by buffalo, eaten by a crocodile, or murdered by bandits; but I certainly couldn't promise this. My entire earnings to date averaged about 10p an hour and would probably only stretch to a week in Bournemouth, and this was not what I had in mind at all. No, what I needed was a job that involved travel, and not round the cities of the Midlands either. I needed a real, abroad type travel job, and I set about finding one with vigour.

Funny how it didn't occur to me that writing and offering myself to travel companies, to lead expeditions up the Amazon, trekking in Nepal etc. as a fifty year old woman with no experience and only a smattering of school French, might not be a very enticing prospect to future employers; but unlikely as it may seem, I did indeed find employment.

Perhaps a recap as to how I had arrived at this 'desperate to travel' position, and my husband's equally 'desperate not to accompany me' position, might be in order. Also, you have suffered all my work experiences, and are still with me; after all the stress, perhaps you too could do with a little holiday, before we return to work. Though I can't promise that the travelling was totally stress free either.

The first time that I went to that amazing place – abroad – was on a school trip in the early '50s. An enterprising drama teacher arranged a tour of German schools with our school drama productions. I played a non-speaking peasant in Yeats' *The Countess Kathleen*, but the female lead in Chekov's *The Bear*. It wasn't too hard to be the female lead as it only had three characters, and the other two were male. This production had caused a frisson of excitement at school, not only because these joint annual productions crossed the boundaries clearly set out by the large double doors between the boys' school and the girls' school, but because in *The Bear* a kiss was called for. Oooo dear we couldn't be having that now could we? Lengthy negotiations could not budge the headmistress; it was vetoed. A chaste laying of hands on the outer edges of upper arms was negotiated – no more. She stopped that, but she couldn't stop this romantic moment. We performed in schools and then stayed at the homes of our hosts. Very handsome head boy Wolfgang was on stage after the performance to give a speech of thanks, he followed it by turning to me and saying;

"… and would you come home with me?" I ignored the laughter from the audience – romantic moments are few in life, and to be treasured.

Another romantic moment treasured from school days occurred at the 'Oh so important' school dance. Mr Wrong had just asked me for the last dance. Taffeta dress rustling in agitation against matching taffeta dolly bag, I tried to think what to say – difficult to do for any length of time as obviously only yes or no were options. Then – Mr Right manfully shouldered his way between us, "Sorry Brian," he said, "she has promised this dance to me." Oooo … er… how romantic is that? He walked me home too. Unfortunately it turned out that we had nothing at all to say to each other.

I remember what I spent my first teaching pay cheque on – a Dansette record player, and Lonnie Donegan's, 'Rock Island Line'. I liked it a lot, but one record was a bit limiting. I couldn't really afford a lot more and so answered an ad in the paper and bought a whole pile of records – crackly 78s, some of them one sided; recordings of the Nuns' Chorus, and Laurence Olivier delivering Hamlet. Not quite what I really wanted, but … I was saving up for the trip of a lifetime. My friend, yes I was still shamelessly associating with my 'air-hostess to be' friend, and I were going to go abroad – on our own. As if that wasn't enough, we were going on a scooter that with a bit of help from her parents, she was going to acquire. We had saved up £60 each to cover all expenses, and were going to spend six weeks scootering around Europe. It was almost unimaginably exciting. This, in the '50s, got us front page headlines, article, and photo in the local newspaper. Remember, travel, like sex wasn't discovered till much later. This was seriously daring stuff. What would you have to do now to get that sort of press coverage? Climb K2 with your granny and her dog? Walk the whole of the Great Wall of China carrying a panda?

We flew from Lydd airport – with the scooter! Imagine trying to get a scooter through security at Heathrow – perhaps if it was in a transparent plastic bag …? I noted in a diary that I kept of this momentous and epic journey, that Lydd airport was a, 'lovely place'. Mmmm … when did I last think that about an airport? The scooter was collected from the car park – grass – for us. We were called by name from the departure lounge, and oh the excitement of a first flight – buckling your seat belt – straining to catch sight of something out of the window. We were also interestingly, the only females on board – that is, not only in the cockpit, but cabin too.

The plan was to travel down through Belgium, France, Italy, and back through Switzerland, Germany and Luxembourg. We clutched our exotic new International Youth Hostelling cards. We started with a spot of bother where we lost each other at the Brussels Exposition. Not only was I unable to speak Flemish, which seemed to be necessary, but I couldn't for the life of me remember where we were staying – she had the address. Lucky I found her or I might still be there now.

Something we discovered very early on was that continental youth hostels were not at all the safe havens with parent figure wardens, and walls covered with notices about washing up, lights out, and sock drying facilities, that we were used to. The most amusing thing that had happened to me in a UK hostel was a glimpse of a woman's bottom, the remembrance of which, and accompanying singing of, 'Blue Moon' kept a whole group of us helpless with laughter for many an hour. Then there was the also very amusing time when mistaking someone's loaf for ours, we had dropped it and it had rolled into a dusty corner of the hostel kitchen. Oh yes, we were easily amused in those days. Continental hostels were very different, and offered much more in the way of entertainment possibilities.

The first, in Paris, seemed to be some sort of communist youth camp, in a sports stadium in a rather scary out of town area. Then there was a cute little 'Three Bears' cottage in the woods – one up and one down – water from the well for drinking, and the stream for washing, the notice said. We had it all to ourselves until 10pm when tucked up in bed – boys arrived. One bedroom – boys with no pyjamas – we were clearly going to see more than a glimpse of ladies bottoms – how were we going to cope? We managed. We managed until we got to Milan.

Luckily en route I had decided not to send back our celebratory bottle of wine that we treated ourselves to on arriving on the Riviera.

"Something the matter with this," I had pronounced wisely. "It must be off – it shouldn't taste like this, all … sour." My friend accepted my expertise, I don't think she had tasted wine at all, whereas I reckoned I was a bit of an expert, after all I had wine every year at Passover time. I knew what wine should taste like – very sweet, a bit like blackcurrant cordial.

However we managed to keep out of serious trouble until we reached Milan. This 'trouble' had everything – well, the usual series of wrong and ridiculous decisions, that goes without saying, but it had more than just danger and embarrassment, it had all the ingredients of a romantic novel – young doctors in white coats with stethoscopes hanging out of the pockets, scooters, fainting fits, nuns – goodness what happened?

We arrived in Milan on a bank holiday. We found the hostel, but it was closed until later; we had the best part of a day to fill. Did we go to see the opera house, the architecture, the museums? No. We would sit in the park alongside the hostel and wait. We lay back on the grass and closed our eyes. When we sat up and opened them again, a semicircle of young men and scooters were arranged in tight formation around us. I had seen a similar scene before. Tom cats hunkered down along our backyard wall waiting patiently for our non tom cat to appear. The purpose here being clearly not dissimilar.

We were fed up with this; we had been receiving unwanted attention from young men ever since we had set off, but in Italy it was unrelenting and we had had enough. And we couldn't understand why … why wouldn't they leave us alone? We were just a couple of unaccompanied, pretty, twenty year old girls, one petite and blonde, one dark and buxom. We were on holiday, so naturally we were wearing our holiday clothes, and it being hot, obviously our holiday clothes were skimpy sun tops, tiny shorts, and rope sandals; what was the attraction for goodness sake? It was a mystery to us. For anyone young enough to be mystified too, perhaps I should point out that riding your scooter, semi-naked through Liverpool in the '50s would have caused something of a stir. Riding through France, and particularly an Italian city, where girls at that time would have not only been discreetly clothed, but also chaperoned, was a seriously bad idea. Even now, in the centre of either Liverpool or Milan I would not recommend semi-nudity.

The circle was closing in despite our frantic 'go aways'. Busty semi-naked girl in temper – irresistible! No point riding off, they all had scooters too. We were becoming tearful, when, exit from hostel gate, Mills and Boon type hero – good looking, charming, but above all respectful.

"Can I help you ladies?" He enquired very, very, politely. Was that a little click of his heels? He was German? Thank goodness. We explained that we were waiting for the hostel to open. Our other predicament was clear to see. The hostel warden was his uncle he told us, adding to his already impressive credentials – i.e. he was not Italian, very handsome, alone, and now connected to respectable youth hostel official. He had, he said, an open topped car nearby, would we like to put our scooter in the hostel grounds and accompany him on a little light sightseeing of the area? Well, yes, we would. The Italian youths knew defeat when they saw it and slunk away.

"… But the hostel … we'll need to be back at …"

"Don't worry," he soothed, "it will be fine."

Well after all the hostel warden was his uncle, of course it would. Wrong again. After a delightful, breezy tour of the bank holiday hot spots of Milan we arrived, rather late, back at the hostel. It was full.

Consultation with his uncle, if it was his uncle, bore no results. Could he possibly have persuaded his 'uncle' to shake his head like that? Was he actually enquiring about spare bed capacity? Perhaps he was asking him if he knew all the words to the German number one hit record. The upshot was that it was now far too late to make it to another hostel, and the chances of finding another bed on this holiday weekend were slight. Our new friend was full of apologies. He was so, so, sorry, this was his fault – but he had an apartment in the city that he shared with his brother. His brother was currently out of town – would we like their two beds and he would sleep on the settee? Well as propositions went for two young girls it sounded a bad one, but it was late, we had nowhere to stay, he had been unfailingly polite so far; there were two of us and only one of him, and he was not Italian. As it turned out he was Italian – just a polite, non predatory Italian, well I supposed, there had to be a few sprinkled through the whole of Italy.

We needn't have worried. We had a nice evening out, at a local restaurant with him and a friend he'd rustled up, and we did indeed sleep in the beds, and he did sleep on the settee. Would girls today see anything to be concerned about? Perhaps not. But this is now, and that was then. In the morning, his marble lined, chandeliered, bachelor apartment boasted not a scrap of food, not even the wherewithal for a cup of coffee. He wanted to take us out for breakfast … or he could go out and get some breakfast.

"Thank you, but no, really we must get going."

To be honest we felt a bit in his debt. We had been wrong to suspect that he might pounce on us; he had taken us out for a meal, and been a charming host and perfect gentleman, and here we were standing in his elegant, luxurious, city apartment in our beach clothes; we would set off and breakfast when safely out of sight. We bade him a fond farewell.

You know how it is when you are looking for somewhere to stop – "there's a place – oh passed it now – what about that one? Looks a bit scruffy – look, there's one! Oh can't turn round now, it's a one way street." Before long there weren't any cafés, as we found ourselves en route to the motorway that was to take us to our next stop – Lugano. A bread shop! Oh passed that too. We were quite hungry and thirsty now, but here was the motorway. Perhaps there would be a motorway service station – there wasn't. Soon it was very hot and the lack of even a drink of water that day was taking its toll. Then suddenly, a sharp pain – looking down I could see a bee attached by its sting to my rope sandalled foot. I instinctively leaned down to swat it off. We careered wildly about the motorway, coming to rest finally on the grass verge, where I immediately fell in a dead faint on the grass. Was this the faint I had waited for all those years ago in the maths lesson? If it was, it was very late. It was not quite so dead as to miss the sounds of brakes, as half a dozen cars screeched to a halt. There seemed to be a bit of a tussle among the drivers over my prone body. Finally one was decided on. Would people fight in order to go out of their way to help here? I doubt it – even if it was a twenty year old female. I felt a bit ashamed of my dismissal of all Italian men, as un-chivalrous. I was bundled into the back of some strange man's car and driven off at terrifying speed, to who knew where, while my friend desperately tried to keep up. I was delivered by this kind gentleman to some sort of convent hospital.

Nuns came out to take delivery. There was a general horrified intake of breath. A large sheet was brought out, and with much tut tutting, and slapping of my chest, legs, and other bare bits, I was bundled into it. I was laid on a bed, sheet tucked firmly under my chin and toes. Several charming young doctors in sparkling white coats gathered round to carefully unwrap me, and share the arduous task of dressing my bee sting. A nun gave me an injection, then another came towards me with the obvious intention of giving me another – the same injection again? Frantic waving of arms to indicate no – or was I just indicating that I was hysterical? I don't blame myself too much. I'm pretty sure that even if I had a basic knowledge of Italian it wouldn't have covered – 'a nun has already given me a tetanus injection, so if that is what you are approaching me with – I don't need it.'

By now it was early afternoon, and we had still not had even a sip of water.

A nun who spoke a little English approached. "Have you eaten today?" she asked kindly. We were too ashamed and embarrassed to admit that we hadn't. "Yes," we lied. What if we had to tell her the circumstances of our, 'not having eaten' – he didn't have anything to eat in his apartment. Besides, we would be out of here shortly and we would go straight to the nearest café; no – "oh it's a bit scruffy" or, "we've passed it now." The very first one we saw.

The question of the hospital bill was beginning to bother us; was someone totting it up now? Services of four nuns, and three doctors – it had clearly been a serious case! One of the young doctors entered the room alone – had they drawn lots? He examined my foot and leg carefully, then my other foot and leg. Checked my throat, eyes and various lymph nodes, and then reluctantly it seemed, announced that we were free to go.

"The bill?" we muttered, "how much do we owe?"

He gave a little bow. "There is nothing to pay," he said gravely, "I have only done what any doctor in Italy would have been happy to do."

Mills and Boon authors – eat your hearts out. I didn't realise it at the time but he was probably only speaking the truth. Anyway this story was not over yet – more Mills and Boon to come, hang on in there – this sort of stuff doesn't feature heavily in my life – honest.

Mid afternoon now, very hot, desperate now, we set off to find a café. We were some distance from the centre of town, then – there was one across the road – stop scooter, let's go. Why am I lying once more on the ground? I never faint, never. But would you believe it, well yes, by now you've probably got the sick bag out ready. Whose scooter screeches to a halt? Yes, handsome doctor still in dazzling white coat with stethoscope hanging out of pocket. He scoops me up in his manly arms and carries me across the road to the café, phones for an ambulance, accompanies us back to the hospital, guesses the problem, and at five o'clock we all eat sandwiches and drink coffee. That's at least 50% of my life's romantic moments, I will spare you the rest as nausea is an unpleasant sensation.

Chapter Fourteen

Travelling came pretty well to an end for a long time after this adventure. Marriage, saving, children, intervened. There was the skiing honeymoon – it took two days and a night to get to Austria overland. This year I have revisited Austria; fifteen minutes to local airport, ninety minute flight – cost, next to nothing.

We settled into a pattern of two weeks in Yugoslavia most summers, interspersed with the odd caravan holiday in Wales, or one year, daily visits to the local baths, pub lunch, and bottle of Martini in the garden afterwards. Funnily enough, that was one of our best holidays. Why Yugoslavia? It was as exotic as I could manage with small children, and we could afford it – £50 per adult head bought a flight, two weeks full board in a reasonable hotel, en suite. We covered the entire coastal area over the years, from Opatija in the north to Montenegro in the south, plus many of the islands. It was nice, but it didn't satisfy my craving for excitement. Except for one occasion that is.

We were sailing out of Split to our holiday destination, Bol on the island of Brac. The water looked choppy in Split harbour, but out to sea it was very rough indeed, and our boat very small. Chairs crashed from side to side of the deck. Glasses and bottles rose up from the little bar and smashed, sending flying glass everywhere, heavy ash trays flew through the air. Most ominously of all, water began to seep in, and wash across the inside decks – we were sinking – we were going to drown. This was not at all the sort of adventure I craved. Much to everyone's relief we eventually managed to put in, at not the right harbour on Brac, but at least some dry land. We were actually, I learned later, reported as missing at sea. Our rep (I didn't realise till much later what an additional nightmare this must have been for her) managed to find a school hall for us to sleep in, and a bit of food. We spent an uncomfortable night, the wind howling outside, and the constant wailing of one woman. "George, I want to go home."

In case I am putting anyone off, now that Yugoslavia is back on the holiday menu, perhaps I should point out that we were travelling early in the season to suit the needs of the two other families that we were holidaying with. Next morning no-one who had been on that boat was willing to board it again, so a coach was rustled up, and we took the equally scary route across the mountains to our resort, on a road that was clearly never intended for anything wider than a couple of goats walking abreast.

How unlucky was the holiday firm 'Yugotours' when Yugoslavia ceased to be a holiday destination and became a war zone? About as unlucky as the diet supplement firm whose product was called 'Aids' I reckon.

I didn't actually crave death, either in a war zone or at sea. I just fancied a bit of spontaneity in my travels. Occasionally it came my way.

Phoning now grown up son on a Friday evening to fix up meeting arrangements for Devon coastal walking holiday, starting on Monday, I mentioned that the holiday programme I had just been watching had mentioned cheap flights to Turkey – did he fancy going to Turkey instead? He did. Monday saw us at Heathrow instead of Minehead. We had, I thought, a good holiday; saw Cappadocia, Pamukkale, ruins, coasts, lots of interesting bus trips; had no major mishaps – well there was that one night that we slept on a bench, but all in all it was a very civilised trip. How strange then, that he has never expressed any interest in travelling with me again.

One problem I didn't have on this trip was unwanted attention from men, or even, any attention from men; for some reason it is not a problem when you are in your late forties. My son however had a lot of attention from men. Presumably in, 'clearing the ground' mode, they were very curious about our relationship. Added to our general oddity as travel companions, we shared a room – well there was no point getting two rooms. The general consensus seemed to be that I, despite all indications to the contrary, must be very rich and that he was my reluctant toy boy – perhaps they could provide some welcome distraction? It was only on the last day that someone managed to figure it out correctly. I don't suppose Turkish men backpacked with their mothers much.

The start of the real damage though, the first nip of the seriously infectious travel bug, began on another occasion, and again by chance.

'Ladies lunching' after my weekly philosophy class. (I went to that class for two years, enjoyed it, took a lively part in the heated discussions, and can remember not one thing about philosophy or the philosophers – not one.) I commented that the next-door travel agent had flights to Almeria in Spain for £50 return from our local airport. I have just been complaining that our recent fares to Austria were originally £8.99, but had now gone up to £12.99. But in those days, the '80s, £50 was cheap.

"Leaves on Sunday – three days time, do you fancy it?" I said playfully to a friend.

"OK," she said, "let's go." So we did.

Flushed with triumph at actually arriving in Almeria and having booked into a small hotel, we set off to explore. Later returning to the hotel we had one of those – 'If I don't laugh soon I will explode,' moments. I had had a couple before – sitting in the centre of the crowded school hall on parents' day with no means of escape, while the first year violinists, 'we've only been learning for a term so we're doing quite well really,' scraped and squeaked and played wrong note after wrong note. Suppressing that wave of rising hysteria was of an altogether greater magnitude than scary science mistress writing on blackboard – 'a week old tadpole swims actively about' – weak old tadpoles ... swimming actively about! Intensive suppressed giggling – but not too much; this was the teacher who told us firmly before the lesson on the reproductive system that nobody, but nobody, was going to find what followed amusing. What would have happened if we had? Head on stake probably. It is this knowledge that you really dare not laugh that makes it so hard not to.

Returning to our hotel, we found that neither of us had the room key; must be at the desk – no, it wasn't. We assured the grumpy, soon to be grumpier woman at the desk that we had never had a key. Everyone looked again. Why the problem? Give us the spare key. Amazingly even for a two star hotel, perhaps especially for a two star hotel, there was no spare key. Angry Spanish woman marched with us to the room, and getting angrier by the minute, proceeded to attack the lock with hammer and chisel, knocking lumps off door and frame in the process. We watched, speechless. At least we were now in the room. We thought we had better stay, in case she set fire to our things, or threw them out of the window. She stamped up and down the stairs getting a new lock, replacing broken tools – her fury gradually bubbled up to a rolling boil. That fatal germ of laughter materialised in our guts. We couldn't laugh, we absolutely couldn't, she would kill us; she had at her disposal a whole bagful of sharp implements. As she crashed about, cursing Spanish curses, my friend tried reading aloud to distract us and soothe her. Unfortunately the passage she chose was spectacularly unsuitable – something on the theme of, the beauty of the calm soul. What made it worse was that during one of our hostess's rage fuelled stomps down the concrete stairs, we moved a bag on the table; the key was under it. Of course we didn't dare tell her, and spent much of the ensuing day pondering the correct moral and practical placement of the key at our departure. Our philosopher friends didn't seem to have covered this precise moral dilemma.

That was day one, the rest turned out to be marginally less likely to send us home with a rupture. No, laryngitis was more of a threat. We calculated how many words were spoken; given that we commenced on waking, at 6 am (early buses) and talked right through non-stop till 11ish – it was quite a lot.

I'm not proud of this, but her ability to jab purposefully at bus timetables, and my mastery of, 'hot and cold water?' and, 'hostel … around here?' got us by. However, in her I had met my match. She managed to get me into a situation that even I would have avoided.

We were in Marbella. It was pouring with rain. We were approached by time-share touts; would I like to see some lovely time-share apartments? No I wouldn't. Instead of walking on, she showed some interest: free trip to apartments, refreshments, travellers' cheques or free meal vouchers, taxi to anywhere you chose after, 'little talk'. I do lots of unwise things, but not these sorts of things. We argued it out over lunch.

"What have we got to lose?" she said. "What else are we going to do?"

I looked out of the window. It was still pouring with rain and we were already very wet.

"Oh all right."

We returned to the time-share touts. There was one little thing that they had omitted to mention. We needed to be single or divorced. This presumably was to stop you needing to consult someone else before signing the contract. Oh no! That was me out – I am a terrible liar, as in can't, rather than can, do it. Even the smallest most innocuous lie causes me great anguish and heart searching. She took a firm grip of my arm.

"Don't worry, leave it to me, I'll do all the talking." She was already twisting off her wedding ring.

Wet and unhappy I arrived at the time-share apartments – we were immediately separated. I was going to have to lie alone. I sat steaming gently by an electric fire, as my interviewer probed my personal circumstances. I could hear my friend at the next table cheerily weaving a complex account of her divorce and subsequent amicable arrangements; he cut her grass, she did his washing; they were still good friends. Perhaps that was why he had run us to the airport, and was at this very moment tending their house and garden, blithely unaware of his newly divorced status. As I haltingly mumbled out details of my own 'divorce' my unhappiness was obviously so apparent that my interviewer leaned forward, put her hand on my knee, and asked kindly,

"Was it a very painful experience?"

I nodded. Not nearly as painful as it would be, breaking the news to my husband that we were now officially divorced, and that I had bought a time-share apartment on the Costa del Sol.

"Look," I blurted, "I don't know if you are paid bonuses for sales, but I have to tell you that I have no intention of buying an apartment, and I really don't want to waste your time when you could be interviewing someone who might." She was very nice about it, and said she was enjoying talking to me, and we could do just that.

Meanwhile my fears were rising for my friend. Having proved to her by some ingenious maths that the time-share would cost her nothing, indeed she would be substantially poorer if she didn't buy it, she had shown such interest that they had brought in a 'closer' – papers were appearing … and pens. What would her husband say if she arrived home with a time-share? He might hold me personally responsible. After all, I was a model of good sense compared to her. I managed to drag her out before any damage was done.

The travellers' cheques. Where were our travellers' cheques? Reluctantly they gave them to us. Why they were reluctant I don't know. They were only valid for holidays booked within the next week through 'Dodgy and Swindle' – an off-shore travel company. Her other 'good idea' had been to bring our bathing costumes and ask to be returned to a hotel a long way away in the hills, where, she had read, there was a brilliant indoor swimming pool … we could say that we were guests, she said. The swimming pool was closed, the taxi had left, we were a long way from town, and it was still pouring with rain. Well, cheap flights did tend to be out of season, and you couldn't rely on the weather in January.

However despite our misadventures, this was clearly someone that I could travel with, and more importantly, someone who was prepared to travel with me. We decided that the following year we would be more ambitious, and travel to Hong Kong to visit a mutual friend who would be living there then. As you could stop off in both directions for no further cost to the flight, why not break our journey in Thailand on the way out, and Singapore on the way back?

We set about saving for this trip by investing in penny shares. This again was her idea. The magazine that she had seen, devoted to making a killing in this field, recommended which very cheap shares were destined to do well. All we needed to do was follow their advice, which was that upon the shares doubling in value – you sold half of them. Well we would sell all of them and there would be our travel money – simple. I remember exactly when I took paper and pencil to our shares and found that sure enough, they had doubled in value – it was time to sell. I'd just have a bite of lunch, watch the TV news and then pass on our personal good news. There turned out to be no good news; the news was very bad – it was Black Wednesday – the day of the stock market crash. Most of our poor little shares never made it; most of the companies went bankrupt, and she refused to sell the few that didn't on the basis of either – you don't want to sell them when they're down, let's wait for them to go up, or, we don't want to sell them when they're doing well.

The lack of travel money wasn't the only problem. As booking time drew near, my friend decided that she really wouldn't be able to manage such a demanding trip because of various bits of her body that were not fully functional. What was I to do? I either went alone or I didn't go at all. The thought of going all that way on my own, in the '80s, before backpackers were two a penny; before gap years, and certainly before it was common for women of any age never mind 'elderly' women, to travel alone, was very scary. But the thought of just abandoning the trip would, after all the anticipation, be a huge disappointment. These places now seem pretty standard travel fare, but then they seemed an almost impossibly exotic opportunity for a mere mortal like me. I would press on.

If people thought I was unwise, at least most of them kept it to themselves, but I was due to go with my lapsed travelling companion to Turkey within a week of my return.

"What if you get killed?" She wailed, encouragingly. "What if you are knifed in some back alley? What will I do about the Turkey trip?"

Through gritted teeth I gave her my dispensation and blessing to go without me.

"But the others?"

There were two other women going too.

"Well my death isn't going to affect them – just go – there'll be three of you won't there?"

I began to notice that I was talking about my imminent demise as if I too thought that it was a foregone conclusion.

"But your funeral," she persisted.

"Miss it," I snarled.

"I'll be too sad to enjoy Turkey," she said mournfully, already sad at the prospect.

Well that was going to be her problem. I had my own. I was seriously scared. By the time departure approached I was just looking forward to setting off in order to set in motion my return home – in any condition, but preferably alive.

Chapter Fifteen

My first stop was Thailand. What a culture shock – how hot it was – how jet lagged I was. I had opted to save money by taking the local train from the airport into Bangkok. This was a brave decision for someone new to Thailand and travelling alone. I was one of only three tourists on the train. They, as I was soon to discover about all other independent travellers, were young. No doubt they were not so surprised at the 'sleepiness' of all the people lying in piles on the train floor, or the people by the side of the track cooking chicken in the dirt by their vending carts. Staying away from vending cart chicken was not a problem. I found myself knocked out by the heat and dehydration, and why had someone advised me that it was easy to travel in Thailand? Hadn't I just queued for twenty minutes to make a phone call, baht in hand, to discover that there were several baht coins and only one fitted the phone boxes – needless to say, it wasn't mine. It was a bit irritating too, to discover that the overnight train that I had booked to Chang Mai in the north, actually passed and stopped at the airport. Still, you couldn't get everything right.

My carriage companion on the overnight train journey was seriously alarmed by my lack of anything to eat. She pressed me with increasing vigour to share her food. With increasing alarm, I refused. I had read about people on overnight trains who fed you drugged food and then robbed you. She turned out to be a very erudite professor from Bangkok University.

When I got to Chang Mai, I was 'lucky' enough I thought, to be there for Songkran – the water throwing festival. This involves buckets of cold and dirty canal water being thrown over passers-by, tourists particularly, as often as possible; and it was possible very often, as bucket wielders lined the streets elbow to elbow. Despite the heat, your body had just warmed up one bucketful of water, when the next cold deluge engulfed you. A streaming cold ensued.

From Chang Mai I had booked a trekking trip to visit the hill tribe villages. Again, pretty run of the mill now, but not then; it was cutting edge stuff. I was nervous. Was this yet another of my huge mistakes? All the others in the group were in their twenties or thirties. Would I be able to keep up? I needn't have worried. At the top of one hill, the guide and I stood alone. He gathered me to him, and addressed the red faced, panting stragglers, toiling towards us.

"This woman is fifty," he announced, his English clear as a bell, "look at her ... and look at you!"

My first thought was – how did he know? Ah yes, the forms we had had to fill in. Was this my proudest moment? Well certainly one of them – I could cut it.

Later ... that night, I wasn't so sure. I lay on the raised floor of a wooden village hut, between two strange men, pigs snuffling below us, chickens clucking, discussions about numbers one and two being bandied about. Smells strange to me, and equally unknown and mysterious substances changed hands. I'm a suburban housewife I thought hysterically – what am I doing here? Numbers one and two were only familiar to me as child potty training terms, and I didn't think this was the same somehow.

Later, on, 'bamboo lashed together raft' trip – very scary due to low level of water meaning that we were constantly being menaced by sharp upward pointing objects and jagged rocks, plus, as our rafter told us cheerily, he had never done this before; we discussed occupations. This brought a rather embarrassed 'actor' from the man that I'd been sleeping next to last night in the hut.

"Yes," chirped his girlfriend, "and he's just starting in a new TV police series – he might be famous."

"Well, what will it be worth?" I asked him, "not to sell my story to the tabloids:

'I slept with X – our steamy night together in Thai drug den.' He looked vaguely concerned – well probably not sure that he would be famous, or that I would do it. He was and I didn't.

By the time I left Bangkok I had learned a lot. Don't get irate, it doesn't help, and just horrifies people. The note telling me that my hill tribe trek was to be a day shorter, as some people wanted to get back earlier, had sent me hot foot to the trek office – what did they mean? They couldn't do this! My annoyance clearly alarmed them – sit down, have a drink of water, your money back, anything, just calm down.

Secondly – that people will tell you what you want to hear.

"Do you know where this hotel is?" Tuk-tuk driver looks at address scribbled on piece of paper.

"Sure." Several circuits of Bangkok later, it was clear that he didn't.

Third – be prepared to adapt. I could have accepted the hotel he suggested on the first circuit rather than the last.

Fourth – Don't go into the Oriental Hotel, or any other of the world's top ten hotels, wearing a crumpled skirt, tee shirt, and flip flops; and with a rucksack, streaming cold, and ankles decorated by circlets of purple bites. You will be followed through the foyer, but won't be approached with any offer of service – so no, you will not be able to treat yourself to a cup of coffee on their terrace.

I had also come up with a workable 'woman travelling alone safely,' strategy. Get up and out early. Eat early in the evening either in your hotel or nearby. The eating alone was a problem that I never quite solved. Best I could do was a book. The problems that I had foreseen however, I had got completely wrong. It was not when things went wrong that you wished you had someone with you. It was great not to have anyone saying,

"I said we should have … I told you not to … that's another mess you have got us into …" No, it was the no-one to share that sunset, or funny moment, or dinner that I missed.

Hong Kong, friends, nice apartment, cucumber sandwiches at the club, dining out in style, trips out to the islands, up The Peak, was an altogether different experience.

My friend in Hong Kong and I, had decided to do a side trip to China. Funnily enough it had seemed to be easier for me to get the relevant information needed for this trip from my local library in England than for her to get it in Hong Kong.

We flew into Guilin. Despite this being a relatively touristy area, the culture shock was huge. First there is the always disconcerting – can't read or even guess what anything says. We got a local bus to our hotel. How would we know it? How would we know when we were there? Nobody on the bus spoke English – why would they? My friend had booked us into a smart international hotel, so that was alright. Chinese food not having the same novelty for her, I remember we ate bizarrely in the hotel's Italian restaurant. Inside the hotel it was all very western and within our comfort zone – outside I was at a loss.

Groups of blind beggars busking, a pig tied to the back of someone's bike, a curious crowd gathering when we stopped to buy some oranges weighed out on a hand held scale in the street, or to look in a shop window. The strange assortment of shoes that looked as if they were a consignment from a charity shop's clear-out – glittering sandals, lace ups, plastic paddling shoes. And above all the spitting, everyone spitting, everywhere. Will they be spitting all over the mock Tudor villages that I gather are being built there now, or the smart shopping centres? I doubt it. I think China is a very different place today.

It was very cheap for us even with the two tier 'them and us' pricing, and special tourists' currency, but difficult to keep track of the huge numbers involved. We once bargained for tee shirts – yuan were knocked off and put back on – a line was drawn in the sand – we walked away in a huff; we'd show him we weren't to be ripped off. Then we worked out, it was 19p he was asking. I'm ashamed to say that embarrassment at our own behaviour prevented us from going back.

I didn't at first understand the significance of the rows of pots of boiling water outside the ... what were these places? Nor did I understand the purpose of baskets of snakes, turtles, ducks, and furry creatures trailing broken legs, that were lined up in front of them ... were these pet shops? No they weren't. Restaurants didn't dawn on me till later. I wish I could forget. Though is it any less cruel to choose your live lobster or fish and have it popped into a pot of boiling water where you can't see it I wonder?

The trip down the river Li is gorgeous, and interesting – conical limestone hills on every side ... so beautiful; just like the pictures I had seen. Fishermen in little boats, using cormorants to catch the fish ... watching riverbank life. Instead of returning straight away to Guilin as most tourists did, we decided to spend a few nights in Yangshou – the end of the boat ride. No international hotels here but clean rooms, mosquito nets, flasks of boiling water for making tea and washing – more my style of establishment.

We had a fascinating couple of days cycling round the surrounding villages. There was blossom on the trees, and the sound of children singing drifting out of schoolroom windows. Women with babies strapped to backs and fronts, despite the 'one child' rule, were everywhere. We 'lunched' one day on Polo mints and 'mystery' cakes, on a hillside watching a rice paddy being ploughed by a man with water buffalo. The sky and surrounding hills were reflected in the still water. There was no sound. It was so beautiful it brought tears to the eyes.

The sparsity of lunch was a result of us thinking that we could pick up something at some shop en route. Shops were hard to find, and when we eventually did, and the proprietor sleeping on a bench had been shaken awake by his tiny child companion, there was nothing to buy – a few dusty combs and tins, and things we didn't recognise. Thoughts of crusty rolls with ham and wholegrain mustard faded. We bought some grey looking cake/biscuits – they tasted disgusting but we had nothing else. We realised afterwards that food here in villages was not inside shops, it was outside, growing or running around.

Later, caught in a sudden deluge, a charming family invited us into their house to shelter. We sat in our dripping cagoules, giants perched on tiny stools, surrounded by diminutive, awe struck adults, and nervous children. We couldn't communicate in any way; we smiled ... then I had an inspiration. I pulled out the biscuits, they wouldn't be strange to them, they were probably a luxury. Their horrified drawing back and vigorous refusal didn't seem to have anything to do with politeness. We reckoned that we had bought some sort of animal feed, perhaps cattle cake. What the Chinese would make animal feed from, well I really don't, even now, want to go there.

We visited markets where medicine men laid out their wares, pulled teeth, or explained the properties of the bears' paws on sale – oh dear. We peeped into a house where a baby was being bathed in a galvanised bucket while grandfather accompanied the proceedings on his violin. Then there was:

"See that man down there? The one lying on the quay."

"Yes."

"He hasn't moved for an awfully long time."

We watched him carefully – he didn't move – he was very wet – he was dead; obviously pulled out of the river. Death is such a no-no to us that we were fascinated. People just walked round him without a glance. Eventually someone came and measured him up, then someone brought a box and, literally, carted him away.

We ate in tiny western style cafés, though not at western style prices. At one we noticed that our meal and the following lengthy, liquor sampling session had cost us 50p; I can't remember if that was each or the total bill. We breakfasted at Joanne's café. Joanne took our order and then disappeared for a long time. She disappeared for a long time the following morning too. Then we noticed her coming out of another café carrying plates. She spoke English – it turned out that she had just opened her 'café' – had no food, facilities, or experience, but was desperate to make some money to travel abroad to study.

Back at the airport, I sent my friend off with our remaining 12p to see what she could get – three non cattle cake biscuits – she had done well!

Funnily enough when I tell this particular friend that that week in China was one of my very favourite travel experiences, she always seems to need a bit of prodding before she agrees. Perhaps I am getting a little paranoid.

On leaving Hong Kong I had allowed a whole week in Singapore because she liked Singapore and thought that she might come with me. In the event she said that she couldn't ... mmmm?

I didn't like Singapore at all, it wasn't and still isn't my kind of place: too modern, too organised, too much traffic and concrete, and much too much emphasis on designer shopping. I did find one shop that I liked though, tucked away down a side street in the Chinese quarter. It was a shop that sold paper goods ... for the dead. My favourite was a lovely paper ship. I suppose it was meant to carry you to wherever you were going, hopefully not catching fire when you arrived. But what I really loved were ... the lifeboats! You are already dead remember ... the ship sinks ... where are they going to take you?

I have cut out and treasured an advertisement for a clock: 'Guaranteed accurate to less than a second in ten million years.' I have always worried about how you would return it if in nine and a half million years, it lost a second. Now I know – hop in the paper boat.

I did manage to find a small characterful Chinese hotel where the following took place. Returning to my room after my 'Singapore Sling' at the Raffles Hotel – clean, tidy etc. this time. I found my bag and all the clothing inside it crawling with thousands of tiny ants. Forgetting my 'don't get angry' lesson, I stormed down to find someone to complain to. I was assured that the rooms were regularly sprayed – so that accounted for the stains on the walls perhaps, but somehow I wasn't appeased. What if there was something else. Something I hadn't found out about yet. I enquired testily:

"Do you have cockroaches?"

"What?" A look of incomprehension.

"Do you have cockroaches?!"

"You want cockroaches? ... Why?" She would never understand these crazy foreigners.

A couple of days of Singapore was enough. I got a local bus over the strait to Malaysia, and Johor Baharu. I spent the day looking round, and visiting the market. Here among the Muslim women with their modest dress and covered heads, I saw a youth sporting a tee shirt graphically adorned with a large smiling penis and the proclamation – 'Don't be daft, don't be silly, put a condom on your willy.' Did he know what it said? He was quite happy to pose for a photo.

After a night watching rats scurry over adjacent, window level, roof tops, and waking up to find a silver fish and its two small insecty companions in my bed, I moved on to a small town that promised an interesting waterfall and park, and hopefully a better hotel.

"Take me to the best hotel in town." I commanded the usual welcome committee at the bus station. A group of them accompanied me there; they must have been impressed. The 'best' hotel in town however, was disappointingly scruffy.

"I want your best room," I demanded at the reception desk. Well sometimes you've just got to splash out haven't you? We all trooped up to an undoubtedly huge room, and it even boasted a television; but all the chairs – rows of them – what were they for? It was used as the town TV room in the evenings it seemed – but that was OK wasn't it? No it wasn't.

Back to Johor Baharu but mercifully this time I found a clean, modern room, in a clean modern hotel. I was learning that when it came to accommodation, although old, quaint and characterful, often looked fine during the day; modern, soulless, and clean usually seemed better at night. It was here, that so near to the end of the trip, and a record free from huge mistakes, I besmirched my clean slate.

I had worried about unwanted attention from men, but this had really not been a problem. Why would it be? A scruffy, large boned, fifty year old, westerner – hardly a threat to the dainty, immaculate, local girls. Besides if I ever felt threatened, or thought, ludicrously, that I was looking too attractive, I had developed a limping, deranged, 'mad woman' look. It was surprisingly easy.

But on that penultimate evening, I had scrubbed up, dressed up, and was feeling relaxed and pleased with myself, as I waited to cross the road from the hotel to the restaurant opposite. A sudden tropical downpour meant that even crossing the street would have soaked you to the skin. I waited alongside a man in a smart suit, Malaysian businessman I guessed. We exchanged a few words about the weather – his English was good. After a pause:

"Would you like to join me for dinner?" he asked.

"No thank you." I prepared to follow through into mad woman mode – not necessary, he went back into the hotel – good. After a few more minutes I went back to see if they had an umbrella at reception; he had just been given the last one.

"May I at least escort you across the road?"

Well, it would have been churlish to refuse. Oh, what the hell – when he asked me to join him, again, I said yes. But on one condition – I pay for myself. This settled we entered the restaurant.

I didn't understand Malaysian restaurants as it turned out. There was a glass case with lots of different food in it. I chose three or four different things. If he was surprised he didn't show it. We were shown to a table, he held the chair for me, and went to get some drinks. It was then that I discovered that I didn't have any money. I had been counting out the bits of different currencies that I had left, on my bed – dividing them into neat piles, and that's where my Malaysian currency was ... on my bed. While I pondered on this dilemma, the food arrived. Unbeknown to me, each of my food choices was the basis of a meal. Squeamish at the best of times about being faced with too much food, I watched in horror as the table and a hastily drafted in side table were piled high with food. That's when he began to tell me how his wife didn't understand him. He worked for the government; he had a car, after our meal we could go on to a nightclub. Oh no we couldn't. He probably thought that someone with such a huge appetite for food might replicate this in other areas.

I was still trying to work out how I could get to my money without taking him to my room ... and bed. I didn't think in the circumstances, that mentioning the word bed in any explanation of my predicament was going to be a good idea. I finally opted for the, 'let's just get the hell out of here approach'. I bet his wife did understand him, it would serve him right if he had to pay for my four meals anyway.

"Ooooh," I yawned, "sorry but it's late, I'm too tired for nightclubbing – time for ... er ... bed."

Damn, damn, that hadn't come out right at all. I think he was too surprised to notice my introduction of what looked like an invitation to bed – it was about half past six. Well, really tired anyway ... but not thinking of bed ... oh no ... not bed.

Well what about tomorrow? He and his car would still be here – we could go for a drive round. Not with my suddenly remembered incredibly early start. I bolted for freedom, and trembling slightly from the exertion of taking the stairs two at a time, wedged a chair under my door handle.

So as you can see I handled travel really, really well, was very sensible, and was now looking for a job helping other people to manage as well as I did.

Next day though, my last, the previous night's farce fading, I sat in the gardens of the palace at Johor Baharu, gazing across the strait. The tour buses with the passengers who never ventured more than a few yards from the safety of their vehicles had gone. The golden domes of the palace glinted in the sun. Huge butterflies fluttered round me among the tropical plants. With eyes full of tears, I thought – I did it. Also – I will never be on that package tour bus again. Well I wasn't quite right on that score, but you can't be expected to see into the future can you?

I arrived home un-stabbed, un-raped, un-mugged, but as well as the numerous other bites I sported, I had been well and truly bitten by the travel bug.

Chapter Sixteen

I did try travelling with my husband, or perhaps that should be, he did try travelling with me, and to be fair all the things that went wrong were not always my fault.

As we flipped and dropped with stomach churning terror in a violent storm over the Rockies, en route from Denver to Aspen, we remembered that our friend in Aspen had told *both* of us to 'not get' the prop plane, not to, 'get the prop plane'. We remembered then that he had told us it was dangerous, planes had crashed, people had been killed. We should have *both* listened more carefully.

It was this friend however who had advised us that walking down the north side of the Grand Canyon, about fourteen miles each way with only a torch and the occasional kip by the side of the trail as he had done, was a wonderful experience. Even camping half way down in both directions it had been a trial, but other interesting things had emerged from the Grand Canyon apart from blisters the size of ping pong balls on my husband's feet. Perhaps his gentlemanly offer to carry the tent had contributed to them. That wasn't my fault either, I didn't ask him to.

The water in the Colorado river at the bottom of the canyon was so cold that you couldn't bear it, despite the fact that the air temperature was so hot that you couldn't bear that either. We had had to join the mass of other people in 'The Phantom Ranch' playing cards, drinking Coke, and waiting till the evening, and temperatures you could venture out in. We fared better though than the man who zigzagged into our camp site and collapsed delirious. He had left his family on the rim and thought he could do the whole twenty eight miles in a day: well the Grand Canyon isn't like that.

"Always happening," said the camp ranger, matter of factly. Amazingly, her administered solution of sugar and salts had him on his way in about an hour.

Then there was the American walking this gruelling trail in rubber flip-flops. Years later puffing to the summit of a mountain in the Lake District, there he was again – still in his flip-flops. What are the odds against that?

The rail trip round the entire USA in two weeks wasn't my fault either. I had suggested an east coast rail rover pass. My husband in uncharacteristically adventurous mode had suggested we get the 'All America' pass. True, it was me who had envisaged that you would be able to get on and off as you pleased – you couldn't. It was so booked up that there were no sleeping berths to be had, and we hardly dared get off and break our journey at all, in case we couldn't get back on again. Covering the whole of the USA with only three stops was interesting, but not to be recommended.

The Texas holiday wasn't my fault at all ... really. I had read about Big Bend National Park in a travel article. It is on the border of Texas and Mexico, and so obscure that even some Americans hadn't heard of it. It sounded really interesting and great for a winter walking holiday. After flying across the Atlantic, north to Chicago, then changing planes and south to San Antonio, then hiring a car and driving all day we got to the park and were finally approaching the entrance. A park ranger came to meet us.

"Park's closing in half an hour," he said. "Federal strike."

"When is it opening again?"

Shrug. "No idea."

"We have come all the way from England to see this park."

Shrug.

You might think we had time for a quick look around, but when I say park, don't think flower beds and a few swings – think Wales. We hung around for a few days. It didn't open. We set off on an impromptu drive around Texas. Funnily enough, that was a great holiday ... I thought. It also gave a real insight into what it must be like growing up in some tiny remote, some times 'dry' community, often fifty or a hundred miles from the next, with little in the way of national newspapers or radio or TV, never mind international news. To have never been to your own state capital, to view New York or San Francisco as being as remote as other countries. To view other countries ... well, other countries didn't seem to feature much in day to day Texas life. Scary how US presidents could come from Texas. However people were charming, and we were amazed that, drinking coffee at some plastic clothed table, in a tiny gas station in the middle of nowhere, someone would say,

"Oh, you must be the people who came all the way from England to visit Big Bend."

One night we were staying in a small town that housed a German community – Fredericksburg. My husband wanted to go to the local, Admiral Nimitz museum. I wouldn't quite, rather have my fingernails pulled out, but even a look round the shops for someone who hates shopping, seemed a more attractive option. I would meet him for brunch.

I noticed a tiny shop dedicated to tracing family histories. In the window were some framed examples – a coat of arms, and a family history, for the name – Jennings! With no-one to share my amazement, I couldn't resist going into the shop.

"Are there many Jennings round here?"

"None at all."

"Oh ... why do you have those in the window?"

"It's just a random sample."

I explained my interest. "Take them," the proprietor said, getting them out of the window – "early Christmas present." Never in a million years could my husband have guessed what I would be carrying when I joined him for brunch that morning.

That was not the only coincidence that day. Looking for somewhere to eat our picnic we were invited in for a coffee by some friendly people from a nearby caravan. If your caravan is miles from anywhere I suppose any new face is a bonus. Where were we from? England was usually enough in these parts, but this couple persisted – which town? I usually said near Stratford-upon-Avon, as together with London this was usually as far as was known. No, which town exactly? Turned out they had not only stayed at our local hotel last year, but also commented on how inconvenient it was that the library closed on a Wednesday, when the tourist information centre was in it. Discussing the irritating closing hours of my small local library, in the vast empty wilderness of Texas was bizarre.

I won't forget the amazing starriness of the skies over the McDonald Observatory in the Davis Mountains, neither of which I had ever heard of; or the diminutive Mexicans in big hats dancing with the tall fancily dressed American girls at our hotel; or the tarantula in the middle of the road, or having our car searched in case we had illegal Mexicans about our persons.

We did have some nice cycling holidays. But there *was* the Turkish one. My husband had specifically asked about distances, and road conditions. I had remembered them as OK. They weren't, and we did end up with punctures, and our bikes in the back of a lorry one night, miles away from our destination. But that only happened once. Perhaps he had thought to ask because of the French cycling holiday I'd planned. We flew into Perpignan, and I'd planned to cycle to Carcasonne. It was only a couple of inches on the map; I just hadn't noticed The Corbieres Mountains kind of covered that particular couple of inches. Still, when we did manage to find somewhere to stay, you got huge jugs of free wine with your meal; and I'd never seen rows of deer hooves nailed to garage doors before. You got a really close up view of the local flora too, as you pushed your bike up the mountains.

Perhaps if we joined an organised group, things would be less likely to go wrong. Wrong again.

Well it wasn't my fault the Russian plane that was to take us to and from Cuba was delayed 24 hours in both directions. Or that the bike tour we had really wanted never got off the ground, so we ended up on a sort of 'Friends of Cuba' tour, being greeted at every stop by local communist party workers. Did the toothpaste etc. that we took, ever get distributed, or was I right in thinking that 'local party workers' teeth all seemed to be rather whiter than the average Cuban's. We toured schools and hospitals; a farm where wheelbarrows were being pushed industriously about, but nothing actually seemed to be growing due to the lack of petrol to either drive machinery, or transport goods to the town. This too was the reason it seemed why an armed mounted guard patrolled the orange orchard while the fruit rotted on the ground – no fuel to get the crop to town. Why couldn't local people pick them up and eat them? Ah, because they might pick fruit still on the trees. This Alice in Wonderland logic was picked up too by some of our party. We had quickly divided into two groups. Those who were curious as to how things worked here, and could see both good and bad (and sad) in the status quo, and those who were determined to see only good. This was illustrated well on our 'extra' day. We were watching some children playing in a stream.

"See," said one of the gritty northern councillors in our party, "our children couldn't play in our streams – too polluted." What – all of our streams? And how did he know the status of this stream. Had he unbeknown to us, taken a water sample?

Still at least when something went wrong it couldn't be my fault personally; perhaps organised tours *were* the answer. I couldn't be blamed for someone stealing my husband's underpants out of the side pockets of his rucksack on that flight to Corn Island in Nicaragua. But wasn't it worth it for that priceless moment in the departure lounge before we boarded the tiny plane, when someone popped their head round the door, and said:

"Fred and Ruth – ready for you to board now."

After all you can always buy more underpants – you can't buy that.

Unfortunately it was on an organised tour too, that we discovered the extreme 'fly-i-ness' of central Australia, and how they covered any food before you could get it to your mouth. But it was me who kept getting sick. The tent leaking during that spectacular storm in Kakadu Park wasn't my fault either, and I did agree to spend the next night in a lodge. Yes I know we could have spent the whole four nights in lodges, but I do love camping. Still I did promise on oath – no more camping after that. But what about the fascinating holiday (no camping involved) that I'd organised in North Carolina. We'd spent many many hours listening to Blue Grass music played by amazingly talented local 'pickers' (that's banjo strings, not cotton) in pubs, in the wooden garden shed of a ninety year old lady, and then in the back room of a barber shop in the middle of nowhere. Mmm ... perhaps I like Blue Grass music a bit more than he does.

However I think it was the trip to Sri Lanka that finished him off. I had organised this one too, and I thought it was a great trip. I had shunned the option of a package tour, or your own car and a driver. Your own car and driver? Us! I discovered later that cars and drivers were very cheap. But I'm not sorry; we would have missed all those things that only happen when you do it yourself – on public transport.

The sight of that bus as we came out of the airport shocked even me. It was crammed with, bulging with, people. People stuffed like sardines inside, people hanging on the outside.

"... Be a works bus," I assured my equally shocked husband, who I could see was getting that, 'here we go again' feeling. "Be the last one from some factory – everyone keen to get home," I fantasised. It wasn't a normal bus – the sort we were going to use. It was.

Over the next two weeks we tried different strategies. If you got to the bus terminus early, you ended up at the bottom of the pile with people sitting on top of you. If you got to the bus stop late, you were sitting on other people, standing, or on the outside.

To defer this dilemma we went from Colombo to Kandy by train. Four secretaries sitting near us were off to Kandy for the famous, 'Festival of the Tooth'. We discovered this when we succumbed to their constant offers of food. Oh, we'd heard of the

'Festival of the Tooth'. Why didn't we come with them they suggested shyly? They knew a policeman in Kandy, he would get us to the front of the queue. Why not? We all trooped into Kandy police station. Their friend wasn't ready yet. Why didn't we leave our bags and come back later? We asked our new friends if they would like to join us for lunch. They were delighted. We left the choice of restaurant and ordering to them. We had a great lunch, lots of everything, a spread of savoury food, drinks, ice cream, more drinks. We were clearly being charged local rates because of our companions. The bill for six of us came to £2.50.

We tramped back to the police station and were transported in a police car, feeling very important, to the Temple of the Tooth. There we were placed, with little delicacy, about a dozen or so from the front. We gazed in disbelief. The queue stretched right out of the temple grounds, and right round the large lake, there must have been thousands standing patiently waiting. We stood for a couple of hours in the blazing sun. The queue never moved. We said goodbye to our new friends and gave up.

Annoyingly, chatting to a fellow tourist next day, he told us that he had been passing the Temple of the Tooth on his way to somewhere else when:

"Psst – want to see the tooth?"

"Oh … OK." Quick look and on his way.

Our other train journey took us to a more obscure challenge. I had read about Adam's Peak. You could climb it apparently – it was a kind of pilgrimage thing – and see the spectacle, from the summit, of the rising sun casting the shadow of the peak onto the clouds below. That sounded interesting.

The train broke down every half hour or so. Nobody was bothered; they just sat in a relaxed fashion on the rails – even the couple who told us they were on their way to their honeymoon. I was concerned that we were going to miss our connecting bus. We did, and had to wait for the next. We saw our bus though, it had left the road and rolled down a hillside into a valley. There were conflicting reports ranging from a couple of broken legs to several dead.

We stayed at the foot of the mountain in what could only be described as a collection of huts. But with no electricity and only an outside water supply, we were served an astonishingly good, and sophisticated meal, elegantly set out on the candle lit table. We were duly woken by our hosts in the middle of the night to begin our ascent.

Up steps, it had said. Well yes it was, but there were miles of them, and those 'tea-houses' mentioned, that lined the route. I had imagined something a bit Cotswoldy – gingham cloths, buttered scones and cream cakes, not a few planks with a bit of lino tacked to them, and some scalding hot, fiendishly strong tea, served in chipped enamel mugs.

The real surprise though was the number of people, thousands of them. My vision of a serene and spiritual ascent followed by standing virtually alone on the summit communing with the marvels of nature, was shattered. There was hardly room to stand on the summit, and would real pilgrims really make rude remarks and pinch your bottom like that?

On the impossibly packed bus going back to Kandy, passing wrecked, off the road vehicles, at regular intervals, someone next to me was sick on someone else's sari. With no possibility of anyone moving more than an eyeball or a hand, I marvelled at the dexterity with which towels and garments were passed to and fro and the situation redeemed. Obviously born of much practice.

Our next bus trip was interesting too. At one of the regular refreshment, get blood circulating in your limbs stops, a young man engaged us in conversation. It seemed that he was heading for Polonnaruwa too, where he was to give an English lesson to a group of trainee teachers. His pupils and the headmaster would be so thrilled to see us. Could we see our way to accompanying him? In return he promised to show us round the ruins that we had come to see. How could we refuse? Everyone was indeed thrilled to see us – what a catch we were! We were persuaded to address the fifty or so trainee teachers on the subject, if we wouldn't mind, of 'Life in England'.

Well that's a tricky one. Especially when the main subject of questions from the floor was, our Royal family. They were fascinated by them. Suffice to say that my husband is not a Royalist. Repeatedly I had to put in a:

"Well that's just his opinion," or that most people would think Princess Diana was charming, and Prince Philip was generally fairly diplomatic. Or that I thought that they were wonderful ambassadors for our country – clearly this was proven here. Yes, they did have ... mmm ... rather troubled private lives but ... er ... most people did not share my husband's opinions about them being a total waste of money, his or anyone else's.

We had used Kandy as our base and stayed at a pleasant b&b 'The Drop Inn' each time we were back in town. The owner and his sons became fond of us it seemed. The family had a house in the hills, they would like to take us there – would we like to go? Well, I certainly would. After much changing of dates and times we finally set off one evening. We had no idea how far we were going, and arrived in the middle of the night, me thrusting gifts into the hands of the sleepy and puzzled people who had been roused from their beds. It was obvious that they had no idea that we were coming. Beds were hastily made up for us and we retired. Next morning we found that all the family men who had brought us and whom we vaguely knew, had disappeared and we were now in the care of the family women, children, and grandfather.

The women laid out a sumptuous breakfast for us and watched shyly from the doorway as we ate. The children were bolder, mouths agape at these exotic strangers in their house. We were rather surprised at how exotic we seemed, as Sri Lanka wasn't an island unused to tourists. We had even been asked in the Botanical Gardens if we would have our photos taken with the family children. We were clearly very fascinating. After our grand and solitary breakfast, there was a hurried conference. One woman and grandfather were delegated to take us for a tour round the garden. When alarming blood stains appeared on my husband's white Englishman's socks, leeches were removed and socks washed and dried on a hot stone.

We gathered from the one person with a little halting English, that the men would be back in a few days. A few days! Besides, our experience told us that might mean two weeks. We really had to go we told them, we had a plane to catch. We thanked them profusely for their hospitality, were guided to the nearest bus, and left.

Perhaps the foregoing will explain why I loved to travel, and my husband didn't – or perhaps not. Anyway somewhere along the line I seemed to have blown it. I was travelling on my own now.

Chapter Seventeen

I hope that you enjoyed that riffle through the highlights and low lights of my travel experiences. Perhaps you, while happy for me to have enjoyed them, are equally happy that you could just stay home. Anyway, holidays over now, it's back to work, or rather, looking for work.

What I needed was either a job that paid enough to fund more travels; I didn't need a lot, I neither needed, nor wanted, to stay in smart hotels, or eat fancy food, or travel round in taxis. The trouble was that the only job that I was qualified to do that would pay enough even for my modest needs, was teaching, and I definitely didn't want to do that. So what I needed was a job actually *in* the travel industry. There definitely was a travel industry by this time, the '80s.

I wrote to every travel company that I could find. I suspect that my letters might have caused some mirth.

"Hey, Zac listen to this – fifty year old woman, with no travel qualifications, no travel work experience, no languages, wants to join our worldwide travel team." Cue, raucous laughter.

"Why on earth does she think we'd give her a job?"

"Because ... she ... she, likes travelling ... and has travelled around a bit."

They must have fallen off their chairs laughing, that is if they had bothered to read past the first line anyway.

However just to illustrate the truth in all those irritating sayings like, 'Nothing ventured nothing gained.' 'Try, try, try again,' and 'The Lord helps those who help themselves,' something else came out of all those letters. One, more broad-based organisation, sent me back a nice reply saying that while they didn't need any holiday reps at the moment, they were actually looking for a hotel inspector. Would I be interested in this post? Would I? Wow – what a fabulous job! Of course I would! I had it all worked out within half an hour.

I would arrive at the hotel about mid afternoon. Few notes about the quality of my reception. They would have to be deferential, even to not very smartly dressed people, wouldn't they? Well, they would to get a good mark from me. Inspect my room, afternoon tea, notes on variety of cakes offered, leisurely bath, few drinks at bar, dinner – best to try the most expensive things – wouldn't want people splashing out on birthdays or anniversaries to be disappointed. Perhaps only a half bottle of wine. Give bed a good testing – full English breakfast. I would then write up my notes at some pub, over lunch, or if too stuffed, on a grassy bank somewhere, where I could lie back and let down the zip on my pants a little. Then on to the next hotel.

Sadly, as usual, the reality failed to live up to my dream. You were expected to report on three to four hotels a day. How could you do that? Just check that Basil Fawlty wasn't behind the reception desk, quick sniff of the toilets, and check a few forks for traces of dried egg between the prongs? I was bitterly disappointed. Plus, an added horror. You were to send your reports back – on a disk! This was in the days when computer activity to my knowledge only took place on the premises of IBM and its customers, or in the bedrooms of teenage boys. Apart from the slipped variety, I knew nothing about disks, floppy or otherwise – how you would record on them – what with. I had no idea even, what they were. Home computing for normal adults was still just a twinkle in Bill Gates' eye.

On both these scores then, the job's appeal shrivelled. However I had been invited down to London, so I went. A group of us, selected applicants, were whisked around some top hotels and given half an hour to write a report on each one. It was difficult.

'Blake's Hotel – all the bedrooms are different … very … um … gorgeous … might be good for ogling celebrities.' 'The Savoy … very posh … no, wrong word … expensive?… no … Art Deco touches … in the West End.' Oh dear, would I be any better if given longer?

My confidence had already been shattered at the initial, 'Let's go round the room and introduce ourselves session.' All the others were food writers, hotel inspectors from some other publication, journalists, even a West End theatre director looking for a career break.

Needless to say I didn't get the job. I catalogued the experience in my now bulging file of interesting but ultimately not enjoyable or productive endeavours.

Looking again at the 100% travel job rejections, I noticed that there was one not total rejection. It didn't offer a job, or even any encouragement, but they had enclosed a list of job descriptions; capacities in which they employed people if and when they were needed. I studied the list, and realised the hopelessness of my ambitions. You needed at least one language. If you couldn't speak Spanish, how were you going to sort out problems in Spanish resorts? If you didn't speak French, what use were you going to be on coach tours of France? After all, anything that could be sorted out in English could probably be sorted out by your charges themselves. Could I brush up my rudimentary French? The fact that it was still rudimentary after five years of being taught French at school, did not bode well. I had tried to learn Spanish. I kept recognising chapter four as I came to it afresh with each new attempt. Languages seem to be a talent, like being artistic, or musical, and I didn't have it.

There was one job though that involved foreign, often far flung travel, and although a foreign language was an advantage, it wasn't essential – a cruise ship escort. The reason for this was obvious when I thought about it. No holiday company would put groups of English speaking people on a ship where English wasn't spoken, now would they? And excursions from ships would have English speaking guides too, wouldn't they?

It has probably become apparent that cruise ships were not at all the style of travelling that I had either experienced or envisaged, but a general application form had been enclosed too. I might as well give it a try. To my surprise and delight I was invited to an interview. The more I studied the brochures, the keener I got. They went up the Amazon ... to Alaska ... everywhere. I was desperate now to get this job – and I did! Well they didn't actually need me at the moment but any time soon they would call on me to attend a training course. I was ecstatic. True the pay was only £35 a week and accepting tips was frowned on, but of course you got the cruise didn't you? To be honest I'd have done it for nothing. It was almost perfect. My friends didn't think so.

"But you will have to dress up; you will have to look at least ... respectable." In case the seriousness of this prospect had not been hammered home sufficiently,

"You will have to wear ... skirts ... court shoes ... evening dresses ... cocktail wear." Yes, well, that was going to be a challenge, I knew it.

My usual 'casual' garb of jeans, trainers, and tee shirts, was clearly not going to impress the clients of this company, but I would just have to tidy up my act. The fact was that I possessed no suitable clothing of any sort, never mind evening wear – evening wear! I fought down panic and tried to remain positive. I could sort it out, I knew I could – how hard could it be? Other people wore 'real' clothing. I had a body, I would find 'real' clothing and put it on. 'Be brave,' I told myself.

There was actually another problem too, that was not common knowledge to my friends, and that surprisingly had not arisen at the interview. On my two experiences of sailing – the Adriatic episode, well perhaps that could be excused, but also a slightly rough channel ferry crossing – I had been very, very, seasick. Perhaps, I thought hopefully that it had just been a coincidence, and I had eaten something that hadn't agreed with me. It was ... well ... just, possible. I convinced myself that it had almost certainly been the case.

If you have been paying close attention prior to this, you will perhaps have noticed that nothing in my life, as probably in your life, is ever straightforward. No sooner had I landed my 'almost' dream job, than there was a huge slump in the holiday industry – cruising it seemed being particularly badly affected. They had needed more cruise escorts, but now they didn't. They would let me know if they ever needed me. I was so disappointed. So near and yet so far. I took to phoning every few months to see if the situation had changed. It hadn't.

This was when my love affair with the back pages of *The Lady* magazine began. Every Tuesday found me queuing outside the library to scrutinise the situations vacant. Well I didn't want to be seen actually buying *The Lady* magazine ... it was ... so ... not me.

There they were:

'Nanny wanted to accompany family on three week holiday in the Caribbean.'

'Family travelling through South America need help with four children.'

'Someone to help with cooking and childcare in Tuscan villa in August.'

I seemed to have lost sight of the fact that holidaying with my own children had been far from relaxing, or conducive to seeing anything at all, and why would I want to be reviving my scone baking routine in Tuscany for goodness sake?

Of course, the fact that travelling with children left you no time to relax or see anything was precisely why people were looking for help – seems pretty obvious to me now. I also overlooked the fact that I had no nannying qualifications, and that even in those days before it took a year to get police clearance, I had no references. My children kindly offered to write me a reference, but I doubt whether that would have counted.

I did however initially manage two interviews, and one job offer.

I wasn't all that keen on the temporary teaching job in Madrid, for the obvious reason that it involved teaching, but my husband was *very* enthusiastic about this one. I'd have accommodation, it was a city, there would be civilised restaurants, and decent wine, average sized fly populations, and no possibility of camping. He'd visit me – often.

The interview was on Christmas Eve in London. I had a houseful of people for Christmas, children, girlfriends, the lot. It was not a convenient time, to put it mildly.

It wasn't quite like Barnet – I didn't say the wrong thing. The problem was that I couldn't say anything. To say that I was insufficiently prepared would have been a serious understatement. I didn't know anything much about the new National Curriculum, nor had I given any thought as to how I would organise my multinational classroom. I had kind of forgotten that it was a job that I was applying for, and was looking upon it more as an opportunity to live in Madrid.

Oh, did I mention? I didn't get the job.

I actually got interviewed for, and given, a job in Switzerland. It was kind of house-mother to groups of children, in a chalet, up a mountain. I was to meet the children – in a car of course, and drive them up the mountain to the chalet (I am particularly terrified of driving up steep slopes). I was to do all the shopping, cooking, packed lunches, keep the place clean, and entertain them in the evenings – but during the day the children would be out with instructors, so all the remaining time after shopping, cooking, cleaning, and planning the evening entertainment, would be my own. It neatly incorporated, I realised after I had applied, everything that I didn't want to do. Fortunately for me, but unfortunately for the two nice ladies who were trying to get this operation off the ground, it never materialised.

Then I saw an equally unsuitable sounding position being advertised, but at least unsuitable in a different, more interesting way. This one was in Nova Scotia. A lady riding instructor with her own stables and horses no less, wanted someone to help her with her invalid mother for three months.

"You're crazy!" The usual, by now well practised, Greek chorus of doom greeted my enthusiasm.

"You've got a bad back ... you don't like old people." While I couldn't deny the first, the second wasn't strictly true. I was an old person, and some old people, like me, were very nice. Besides it was only three months. Three months could be a long time, ventured a friend. She was right, but I brushed all this aside. I spoke to the lady on the phone, she sounded nice. She obviously thought that I sounded nice, and the deal was done. It didn't actually pay well. It didn't actually pay at all, and I was going to have to pay my own fare, but once there I would be fed and housed and taught to ride. I'd always fancied learning to ride, and her son was a ski-instructor so perhaps I might even learn to ski beyond the beginners' class, as well. But mainly what I was looking forward to was a chance to sample life in Nova Scotia, a place that I knew nothing about.

The timing could have been better – January – not the most enticing time in rural eastern Canada, but you can't have everything. That wasn't the only bit of bad timing as it turned out. Unbeknown to me as I set out, mother had been simultaneously taken ill. By the time I arrived in Nova Scotia, minus my luggage which was still at Schipol airport, mother was in hospital. Twenty four hours later, she was dead. I did see her ... kind of ... she occupied a small cardboard box on the dressing table in the now spare room, and thus turned out to be no strain to my back, or patience, in fact no trouble at all.

What was I to do? I had just arrived. Elaborate arrangements had been made to meet up with my husband in New York in three months time for our son's wedding celebration. My husband advised staying put, it would be too complicated if I came home. He was prepared for three months of ... I don't know what – freedom perhaps. Should I be suspicious? Certainly, Mary, about the same age as me, was happy for me to stay. She had been very attached to her mother, lived alone now, and would be glad of the company. I could help her in the stables instead. So that was settled. I had gone from geriatric care assistant to stable girl in forty eight hours.

Mary was devoted to her horses and to teaching people to ride – it was her life – it was not a lucrative life though. For the first time I experienced, literally, living from hand to mouth.

"Right," she'd say, someone's riding lesson money in her hand, "that's our supper tonight."

It was strangely satisfying. I had only ever checked figures on bits of paper. You lose the plot somehow with the bit of paper. Her whole relationship with money was so different to mine. I started from the basis, 'Do you really need this – really, really need it,' perhaps wait a month or so and see if you still thought you needed it, and if so, did you have the money? Then if you hadn't totally lost interest by then and were sure you could afford it – then you checked around carefully to find the best price, guarantees, references, etc. and made the purchase. Mary operated on a totally different basis.

A horse has got out and onto the road. I need a gate across the drive – pick up the phone:

"Come and put a gate up." No thinking about it for a while, no checking that she could pay, or ringing round to get the best quote.

If she got a bit of money she spent it immediately. There was always something that she knew she wanted. When we discussed this difference in modus operandi, she thought that I was crazy. Perhaps I was. I'd never thought about it before. Certainly it made me think about my being over cautious. I suddenly realise that this does not seem to fit my perceived persona. But I kept a very safe base from which to venture foolishly out. I rarely took serious risks. While she just jumped, I always checked that the safety net was there. I think this is an inbuilt personality thing. I did try to be more like her but couldn't do it.

I was warned early on by her friends not to try and keep up with Mary. She was tiny, but strong, and with about ten times as much energy as me; but not keeping up with her, was really not an option that I felt I could fairly take. We rose early, bite to eat (standing up) shovel out horse stalls, replace bedding, change water, fill hay troughs, groom horses, saddle horses, exercise horses. Then into town to get food, oats for horses, tack replacements etc. – lunch. After lunch, scrape and paint horse-box, or prune and tie up raspberries – haul late delivery of hay into hayloft. There was always some physically demanding thing that needed doing.

I was used, after a leisurely breakfast to doing one, smallish, thing, having a cup of coffee, doing another, smallish, thing – lunch – rest – doing some very light, afternoon type, smallish, thing – glass of wine, supper, and the evening was for … resting.

Mary, and by dint of me being with Mary … me … never stopped.

I remember the fencing. A man came to replace the field fencing. We were to help him fix the posts and tie the wires. We had already toiled for hours, when I realised with horror that we were probably not going to stop for lunch until we got to the far distant corner. No, I couldn't do it. I was exhausted and hungry. We toiled on – very, very, gradually the corner got nearer – lunch, a sit down, I was desperate. We got there!

"Right, now we'll do this side," Mary said, pointing to the next corner on the distant horizon.

We ate huge suppers, but I never was so slim, and if I had had the time or the energy, or come to think of it, the scales, I'm sure that I would have seen that I had lost stones.

We lived in a typical wooden, North American house, cosily heated by a wood stove. It stood on ten acres of beautiful land sloping down to a river. The walk along the river was so beautiful that it brought tears to my eyes every time I walked it. I took copious photos of my eye-wateringly beautiful walk – it looked … nothing: a river, an estuary, a footpath. What was so magical then? First, it was silent, except for the sound of birds, and sometimes the wind. We hardly ever experience silence on this small overcrowded island. There is always traffic noise, a plane overhead, road works, car horns, a lawnmower. As well as total absence of man-made sounds, there was total absence of man-made artefacts too – no pylons, flyovers, electricity sub stations. Nothing that was not provided by nature – it was sheer magic.

Mary was English, she would have liked, now that her mother had died, to return to England, but her house with its ten acres would not buy even a one bedroom flat in England. She was stuck.

The river was disconcertingly called, The Avon. Disconcerting because Windsor, our nearest town stood on it. The whole island was a conundrum. Halifax was an east coast port near Dartmouth, Liverpool was down south, at least New Glasgow was where it should be, up north.

Occasionally we had days off. We packed a picnic and Mary kindly took me to see some of the sights. I appreciated that, it was kind of her, because I was already bored witless by trailing my own visitors around Stratford and Moreton-in-the-Marsh.

We went to Peggy's Cove, which must be one of the tiniest famous beauty spots ever. Another day we sat waiting for the famous Bay of Fundy bore, between Nova Scotia and New Brunswick, supposedly the highest tide in the world. It had obviously got bored and never made an appearance. That wasn't the only important thing we had. Windsor stood directly on the forty fifth parallel, exactly half way between the North Pole and the Equator, and we had a post to inform us of this. So we weren't totally boonies.

Mary did teach me to ride – well I thought she did. Though don't, she said ominously, ever tell anyone that you can ride. Advice, years later I was to ignore disastrously when I signed on for a week's riding holiday. Beginners would be OK they had said.

"I've done a bit of riding," I said. I doubted whether beginners would get to do that all important galloping across the Northumberland moors, wind in hair, horse's mane flying, that I had in mind.

"Walk to that post, trot to the next, gallop to the next," said the not very friendly Northumberland lady instructor.

"What?" How could I let the horse know all that, I thought. It didn't like me already, I could tell.

I thought riding was the art of staying on. Mary had been a bit over cautious due to my late start in riding, and advanced age, with … 'staying on'. I was good at staying on, and I thought that meant I was a fairly good rider – I wasn't.

But I did learn in Nova Scotia something that 'horsey' people will already know; horses have very definite personalities. There was no mistaking the way my horse 'Lady' simpered and batted her eyelashes when she passed the boys. Or the way that teenager 'Boy' having kicked down his stall door, and escaped to the field, did circuit after circuit, and after each one came panting to the gate where I was standing helplessly watching. The message was clear.

'That's another one … and there's nothing you can do to stop me.'

When five foot Mary showed up, he was immediately respectful.

I had no illusions about the skiing though. My honeymoon had been spent in the beginner's class, ski-wise, while my husband progressed up the ranks.

"I think my job is to follow you around, picking you up," volunteered my Canadian instructor, ungallantly. I was clearly not improving.

I had been met at the airport by one of Mary's friends, it was she who broke the news that Mary was at the hospital, and why. She was a woman about my own age. It was fascinating how on the hour or so's journey back, we said exactly the same things about husbands, families, and life in general, despite our very different backgrounds. Also, she told me, a few of them went to morning classes at the university in the next town. They then had lunch at a local tea room – would I like to join them? Pretty much what I did at home then.

In some ways life in rural Nova Scotia was a step back in time – no locks on doors – keys left in cars – precious little entertainment, well not that I heard of, certainly outside Halifax. People 'got together'. They got together for supper and a chat, or in one friend's house to listen to 'Les Miserables'. I didn't even like 'Les Miserables' before that.

We had a bizarre ritual when we arrived at someone's house. We went immediately to the kitchen sink where we filled our dozens of plastic water containers. We only had well water which wasn't pure enough to drink. So no pleases or thank yous, we just got on with it, while exchanging chat.

Not that everything in Nova Scotia was idyllic, far from it. There was unemployment and poverty too. We sometimes passed through tiny communities of what looked like shacks in the middle of nowhere – what went on there? The first newspaper I looked at, reported the murder of a prostitute who had been found stuffed head first in a rubbish bin. There seemed to be a lot of cancer too, which seemed to have mysterious connections with things that had gone on in the past. People were not keen to talk about problems – perhaps not to show Nova Scotia in a bad light, I don't know. The tax system seemed unfair too. Poor, Nova Scotians paid high taxes on everything they bought, while oil rich Albertans paid little or no tax.

After six weeks I began to feel that my friend had been right, three months was a long time to spend as a guest in someone else's house – a long time for them too. It also seemed a shame to be in Canada for so long, and not be seeing more of it. I thought I would try to buy a rail rover ticket. Planning such a trip was really difficult with no internet, and no library. One of the things I missed most of all was being able to pop to the library to find books on anywhere, or anything, and check things out. There was a library, but it was in someone's front room and open something like Wednesday morning and Friday evening. I never did get to see it. Now of course you couldn't be too remote for the internet, but that was way before the ubiquitous internet. Years later, I met someone in some tiny remote community in northern Nova Scotia who made and sold, period, clay pipes, to film companies, and collectors. How could he possibly operate from this ultimate in remote spots? The internet, of course.

And so I set out one morning from Halifax's little railway station, with its second hand magazine stand, on what was to turn out to be a journey of the best part of 20,000 miles.

Chapter Eighteen

The scale of Canada, even if you already know that it is big, is still hard for someone from such a tiny island to comprehend. The train left Halifax mid day, but it wouldn't arrive in Montreal till next morning. The bright young university student in my carriage was so excited. She had never been out of Nova Scotia before.

A change of train in Toronto's palatial railway station, and heading west now on Via rail for the three day crossing to Vancouver.

An elderly man sitting near me was crossing the continent in order to attend his daughter's wedding in Seattle. We set out at midnight. In the morning he asked the conductor,

"Are we nearly there yet?"

"No, we're not out of Ontario yet."

At midday,

"Are we nearly there yet?"

"No we're not out of Ontario yet."

I can't remember exactly how long it took before we were even out of Ontario but it was a long time, and a thousand lakes later.

I loved the way when the train stopped for water, and fuel, you had half an hour, or an hour, to look round some tiny township, literally in the middle of nowhere, imagining what it would be like to live there. I remember the sinking feeling too, coming out of a station 'ladies', in my 'train pyjamas' with only my sponge bag, and finding the train had disappeared, and knowing too, that they only ran every three days. Fortunately it had just moved up to the water tank.

I felt a bit guilty about money spent on this trip. I hadn't been expecting to make any money at this 'job', but neither was I supposed to be spending large amounts. The rail rover ticket, out of season had been a bargain. Sleeping berths were relatively expensive, as was eating in the dining car, especially for a month. I devised an 'alternative' strategy. The train, apart from the Rockies section, was pretty empty. I commandeered four seats facing each other in pairs. I then spread my possessions and myself over them. I picked up food and drink at train stops. Doughnuts, I seem to remember featured quite heavily in my diet. At night I washed, cleaned my teeth and changed into my 'train pyjamas' – a towelling track suit. I had brought a light blanket (Mary's suggestion) and made a pillow out of clothes. No wonder I looked so smart. Every few days I got off the train and slept in a bed for a night or two, sometimes three. I realise that this arrangement would suit very few people, but for what I got out of this trip it was worth it for me a hundred times over. Indeed I got so used to my modus operandi that when I got back over to the east coast again, and the journeys between Ottawa, Quebec etc. were less than twenty four hours, I panicked. You couldn't 'settle down' on such short journeys – they were so rushed – why, I'd need to get off in only twelve hours.

I broke my journey at Winnipeg and travelled the thousand miles north to Churchill. I love what is called in our house, 'miles and miles of bugger all'. Perhaps you can guess whose definition that is. This certainly fitted the description perfectly. The road petered out, the trees petered out, the telegraph poles leaned and crouched to the brown, scrubby, perma frosted earth. What could have been a boring journey was enlivened, not altogether happily, by large numbers of Inuit who piled their fridges, sofas, whiskey bottles, and colourful language into what, apart from planes, was the only form of transport in these parts.

I was greeted at Churchill with, "What are you coming here now for? The polar bear season is finished." I stood and looked out across the ice, marvelling that there was nothing between me and the North Pole – looked around the frozen frontier town, then back to Winnipeg, and on to the Rockies.

My sister upon hearing about my proposed job in Canada, had said,

"Why don't you call on cousin David, he lives in Canada?"

I had tried to point out that this was going to be difficult as I was going to be in the extreme east, and cousin David lived near Vancouver, but I took his address just to please her. Amazingly, as it turned out, I did get to call on him. I don't think my sister thought that there was anything strange about this at all.

I also travelled down the Skeena River to Prince George and Prince Rupert, back to Jasper, down to Vancouver, and over to Vancouver Island. Here I noted that after all this travel, and being just about as far from home as I could be, the season, indeed the vegetation looked very much as it would be at home.

Before embarking on the long journey back to Nova Scotia, I did what was undoubtedly the stupidest and most dangerous thing, in a long career of stupid and occasionally dangerous things.

I had stopped off for three 'between train' days in Jasper. I was staying with a lovely couple in the spare room of their bungalow – only other guest, local newspaper reporter from Nuneaton. I had sensibly I thought, refused his kind offer of a place on the back of his motor-bike for a bit of al fresco touring. Instead I had walked alone through, 'beware of bears' labelled woods, eaten my lunch in solitary splendour by a mirror-like lake in the sort of impossibly beautiful glade that you see on posters in greasy spoon cafés. But now I would like to see the famous Ice-field Parkway en route to Lake Louise and Banff. There was a bus, but with a contrariness that I thought was wholly British, the return bus arrived back in Jasper half an hour after the train left, meaning another three days wait for the next train.

With the misjudgement for which I am well known, I estimated that as the distance was only an inch or two on the map, it couldn't be very far – I should be able to hitch it. I would of course only accept lifts from women, or couples, preferably with children. I would be very careful, and just see if I could get anything. I should point out here for those as uninformed as I was, that the Ice-field Parkway is a hundred and thirty seven miles long, and that most people allocate at least a day to travel along it as they are mainly holiday makers, and that they are not likely to want a complete stranger as part of their holiday plans for a whole day, or more.

By a huge piece of good luck, or as it turned out, a huge piece of bad luck, I got a lift to Banff easily. A nice lady filling her car at a petrol station in the town, was indeed going to Banff, and was willing to take me back with her. She was returning there after a conference she had attended in Jasper. We got on like a house on fire – she was fun, and kindness itself – stopping while we watched moose drinking in lakes, telling me about the spectacular scenery that we drove through, going out of her way to take me to Lake Louise. We sat in the famous hotel there, sipping coffee while she relayed tales from her tour guide friend, who, when asked the weight of one of the local mountains, by a clearly thoughtful and scientifically minded tourist, answered,

"Would that be with or without the trees?"

She finally delivered me to Banff International hostel, and waited to make sure that I got in OK.

What a perfect day – good decision Ruth.

The next day I paid.

The clear blue sky had turned to iron grey and looked threatening. I walked out onto the through-way, to Jasper. Cars were reasonably plentiful but sped past me – no-one would stop, even to ask how far I was going. No-one wanted to commit themselves to my company all day, why would they? I waited and waited; I needed to get back for the train next morning. Then at last a car with a man and long haired woman was slowing down. Except that when the car stopped I could see that the long haired woman was in fact a long haired man. What was I thinking? I found myself getting in. Partly I suppose motivated by desperation, and partly my old problem – you don't want to infer that people might be rapists or axe murderers. Much better to risk your life than risk offending people. How nicely brought up I was! They could take me as far as Lake Louise they said.

"OK," I found myself saying.

There was a sensible, normal road between Banff and Lake Louise. I knew it. Why then did they have to go via all these little back roads? Why were we bumping over unmade tracks and into the forest? To see their friend, a forestry worker who lived, obviously, in the forest. A likely story, I whimpered inwardly, but as it turned out – true. This should have made me feel better, but wait ... a forestry worker would *definitely* have an axe, wouldn't he? And a chain saw ... and a whole forest for burying bodies. It all began to fit horribly together. They probably thought I needed that cup of coffee we had with their friend. I must have looked decidedly freaked out.

The journey scored ten out of ten on the anxiety scale for me, but they were actually very pleasant young men, and did indeed drop me off unmolested and un-chainsawed, but shaky at Lake Louise.

Never, never, do anything as stupid and reckless as that ever again, I told myself sternly.

As traffic leaving the town could be going in either direction, the men had advised me to get beyond the junction, and onto the road heading only to Jasper. It turned out to be quite a long way out of town, and snowflakes were beginning to fall. I had thought, hard now to think why, that the traffic from Lake Louise would be heavier. It wasn't, there was hardly any traffic, and none of it was stopping. The snow was quite heavy now, and beginning to pile up. I remembered what the two men had said about a bear that had been seen near the road, just outside Lake Louise. It had 'approached' someone. I kept glancing uneasily over my shoulder, though what I thought I could do if attacked, or even, 'approached' by a bear on this lonely stretch of road, surrounded by rapidly deepening snowdrifts, I don't know. An 'approaching' bear was unlikely to be wanting to know the time, or seeking a bit of idle chit chat.

I did actually approach a bear myself once, years later, near Whistler in another part of the Canadian Rockies. I was doing a circular walk, on my own, and was almost home, when I saw the bear on the path in front of me. It had its back to me. I fought down panic by assuming that as its nose was at the far end, it wouldn't pick up my scent. No, not logical, but alone with a bear, logic is an early victim. I froze. Perhaps it would melt back into the forest. It didn't. I walked forward a bit. It walked forward a bit. I walked forward a bit more. It walked forward a bit more. It was clearly doing the same walk as me. I couldn't remember what you should do when attacked by a bear: run uphill? downhill? roll into a ball? shout? freeze? I turned and ran as fast as my wobbly legs would carry me, back the long, long, way that I'd come. I did pause at one point to lock myself in a Portaloo, left helpfully by the track. What if the bear took up position outside? I couldn't assume that it would be just patiently waiting to spend a penny. The thing is, I hadn't seen another soul the whole day, nor had I told anyone where I was going. Well I was only going for a walk, why would I? Starving to death in a Portaloo in a Canadian forest was not a dignified way to go. Perhaps better to be torn to pieces by a bear. I eventually came out, and ran.

"Mum, bears are seriously dangerous, stop messing about," admonished one of my sons, on hearing about my day. There is something faintly satisfying about being lectured by one's children, on the need to be sensible. However lecturing other people on the need to be sensible is a waste of time. They either are, or they aren't, and nothing you can say will make any difference, as events outside Lake Louise were to prove.

The bear outside Lake Louise on the road to Jasper did not appear. Unfortunately neither did any vehicles prepared to stop, indeed hardly any vehicles at all. The weather was getting seriously bad. I was just about to give up and trudge back through the swirling snow, while I could still see the way, and write off another three days, when a van stopped. It contained one man and a load of bread. What was the matter with me? I was getting in. I was going to politeness myself to death. As he was forbidden by his firm, he explained, from picking up hitch hikers, there was no front passenger seat; so I had to sit on the rusty, greasy, spare wheel that occupied this space. Why had they forbidden him from picking up hitch hikers? Was it because *they* suspected that he was an axe murderer, but he was also such an exceptionally good bread delivery man that they didn't want to sack him? I looked around for axes. What if his axes had been confiscated by his firm, but he had learned how to smother people with large loaves?

We delivered bread to several establishments around the Icefield Parkway complex. I suppose I could have got out and made a run for it, but by this time the snowstorm had become a blizzard and there was a total white-out. I had kind of lost the ability to make decisions now, mortified, as each one turned out to be worse than the last. Did freezing to death, as I escaped from the car and stumbled into a snowdrift, sound better than being smothered with a sliced loaf? I was no longer sure, so I stayed put.

He was actually very nice, no thanks to my aforementioned lack of judgement, and had just enjoyed a bit of company, but I staggered out at Jasper and said a little prayer of thanks for my safe delivery from my own stupidity.

"Take care now," he said meaningfully as I climbed, crippled and greasy, off the spare wheel. Even he thought that I was in need of care – psychiatric probably.

I travelled back to Nova Scotia via Niagara Falls, some sightseeing in Montreal, Toronto, and Frencher than France Quebec, and a prison cell in Ottawa – bars, clanking door, the lot – in a prison that had been converted into a youth hostel.

When I arrived back in Nova Scotia to pick up my stuff, a miraculous transformation had taken place. The brown, frozen ground had burst forth into lush vibrant green swathes. There were carpets of buttercups that hurt your eyes with their yellow shininess. There was blossom, and flowers – the fields – my walk, were almost too beautiful to bear. But I had to be off to an altogether different world, New York, and the trendy Hamptons on Long Island, where the re-wedding was to take place.

My travels ended with an eye-opening train ride through the state of New York. We tend to think of New York as Manhattan, but as my daughter-in-law once said,

"You can find anything that you are looking for in New York State." She was right. The Adirondack mountains for skiing, the Catskills for walking, Long Island for beautiful beaches, the historic towns along the Hudson, and what was that sea? I'd asked the conductor, puzzled, was it the Atlantic? It wasn't the sea, though it stretched to the horizon, it was Lake Champlain, and I'd never even heard of it.

It had been a roller coaster three months, and no, it hadn't turned out to be what I had expected, and yes I had been homesick at times, and yes I had got myself into some ridiculous scrapes, but I wouldn't have missed it for anything. I had wanted to travel, and travel I had.

Chapter Nineteen

When I finally got home I found that I had kind of, gone off *The Lady* magazine. But I hadn't gone off the idea of cruising. I resumed my whining, 'Can I come and work for you?' phone calls, until one day. Hallelujah! The answer was – yes.

We were a motley group at the training course. People of all ages, and from many backgrounds, and although there were people from many previous jobs, nurses and teachers seemed to be well represented; we even boasted one representative from psychiatric care. How appropriate that was going to turn out to be.

In due course I was given a cruise group to escort. Well actually I was given two. Oh dear it was agony. How was I going to choose between going to the Canaries with stop offs in Gambia and Senegal, and going to The Baltic, Sweden, Norway, and ... St. Petersburg. They both sounded so wonderful. When I pre-ambled my agony at coming to a decision to my supervisor, there was a short pause. "No," she said, "you don't understand ... I'm asking you to do both of them." Asking me! Both of them! I have never wanted so much to reach down the phone and squeeze someone half to death. I never quite got used to the bizarre nature of these phone calls.

"No, sorry I can't manage South America on the 24th."

"I might be able to do Malaysia on the 7th... Oh ... it's six weeks ... I'll let you know."

Nor could I have imagined that it would get to,

"Oh, not The Canaries again – who got that round Africa trip?"

Even more bizarre were the phone calls when I rang to accept something.

"OK, I'll do Malaysia and Borneo on the 7th."

"Oh, thank you Ruth!"

I never did get used to the grateful thanks. Anyway that was all in the future. When I had stopped dancing and hugging myself in disbelief, I needed to deal with the clothing problem.

In those days we weren't fully kitted out with uniform. We had a jacket and a skirt – yes a skirt – courage woman, and a scarf. The rest you provided yourself, including the dreaded, 'evening wear'. This was before the days of 'casual eating' options in the evenings. People wore seriously formal dress in the evenings. I studied the pictures in the brochures, of laughing handsome men, and laughing attractive women. They were all wearing dress suits, and what looked like ball gowns. They were either leaning on the deck rails holding cocktail glasses, or exchanging banter with the captain over glasses of champagne. I shivered with apprehension. This wasn't a world I related to at all. Had I made another ghastly mistake? And even if I spent a couple of months pay in advance, it wasn't going to get me too many ball-gowns or cocktail dresses. I would have to improvise. Fortunately this was something I was well versed in. I reassured myself with the thought that I, unlike the 'real' passengers did not have to look 'good' or 'nice' certainly not 'attractive'. I just had to look respectable, and not stick out for the wrong reasons from the laughing, cocktail sipping 'real' cruisers. I decided that a long black skirt, black patent shoes, and a variety of tops were the answer. I picked up in a sale a black top that was entirely encrusted in industrial quantities of sequins, only a few of which had dropped off, and could be sewn back on – just the job. Having trailed around every shoe shop, trying unsuccessfully to squeeze my protesting, trainer and flip-flop wearing feet into court shoes, I found a comfy, brand new, pair of Bally court shoes in a charity shop for £2. And how's this for a coincidence? Thumbing dispiritedly through the ball-gown section of a pattern book in my tiny local sewing shop, and wondering if as a very poor sewer I could make a ball-gown in four days, I overheard this conversation:

"Buttons and thread to match this please."

"Mmm – nice material. What are you making?"

"It's a cocktail dress."

"Oh, going somewhere nice?"

"On a cruise actually." The speaker then went on to name the ship, cruise, and company that she was travelling with – it was mine. Feeling as if I was taking part in some reality – 'scare the living daylights out of an unsuspecting member of the public' show, I couldn't resist turning with a flourish and announcing,

"… And I am to be your cruise escort – allow me to introduce myself," or words to that effect. The poor woman nervously checked out the place for hidden cameras, I think she expected some grinning TV personality to leap from behind the rolls of fabric.

The big day arrived. The timing could have been better. It was the day that the council planning committee were to carry out a site visit in connection with our application to build a house at the bottom of our garden. As well as packing my, for me, huge wardrobe, being on the ball for the planners, and trying not to notice the group of neighbours who had gathered at the top of our drive, glaring and muttering angrily, I had, but had, to catch that fairly early train to get to Southampton on time.

What if the planning committee were late, what if they lingered? Was I going to have to choose between new house and new job?

I just made it – I flew lunch-less to the station, lugged with some difficulty, my huge case on board the train, and spent the journey frantically studying my instruction manual. At Southampton I met the other trainee and our experienced mentor. The three of us were doing this trip together.

Onto the ship, introduce ourselves to staff, sort out problems, familiarise myself with ship's layout, stand at top of gangway to greet passengers – and sail away … into force ten gale … in the channel.

"Sail-away party for people travelling on their own," said – I shall call her Ann. "We should attend this, some of our passengers will probably be there." It did cross my mind as I downed the champagne and wolfed the peanuts – I was hungry and thirsty – that I had actually eaten nothing since my pre-inspection, rushed breakfast. From the sail-away party – quick wash and change and into dinner.

The sea was very, very, rough. The ship was rocking badly. It turned out to be a ship that was prone to rock badly; indeed the worst ship for rocking badly that I was ever to come across. I wasn't feeling too well. Still a proper meal would probably settle my stomach. I had barely got past the soup, when the spectre of letting myself, my job, and our passengers down, was overtaken by the more pressing need to throw up. Fortunately I made it out of the dining room; unfortunately I didn't make it to an appropriate place. What was I to do? With hindsight, scarpering incognito would have been an inglorious but understandable and sensible course of action. But, perhaps it was the surfeit of unaccustomed champagne. I headed for the reception desk.

"I've been sick in the corridor – outside the dining room."

"A passenger has been sick," said the kindly receptionist, who I had introduced myself to only an hour before, offering me a helping hand out of my disgrace.

"No it was me," I wailed before sprinting back to my cabin – just in time.

It was a nice cabin, a big cabin, I was sharing it with Ann. It only had one drawback – it was at the front (I will dispense with nautical terms in deference to the uninitiated). Whenever the anchor chain was lowered which was usually at about 6am, there was a heart stopping amount of sudden noise about three feet from my sleeping head.

It was a good job that it was a nice cabin, because I spent three days there. As well as the force ten gale in the channel, the little monkey had got into the Bay of Biscay too, and the Atlantic, and on this particular itinerary our first stop was Madeira. Every time I sat up, never mind got up, I felt sick. Visits to the bathroom were fraught with danger. Even the ship's doctor coming and giving me a seasickness injection didn't seem to help. I lay in agony. It wasn't just the seasickness. I wanted this job so badly, and they would never give it to me now. This was only a probationary trip, and who would want a cruise escort who spends all her time in bed, seasick. I was supposed to be out there helping other people, perhaps even other seasick people. Also, what would I have done if I had been on my own? What, in the unlikely event that I was ever asked to work again, would I do on my own?

Meanwhile Ann came and went. The captain's cocktail party came and went; our own cocktail party came and went. Luckily Ann and my fellow trainee were not affected in the slightest, and were eating, drinking, and having, I was told, a great time. How does this work? How different could the inner workings of different people's ears be for goodness sake!

Finally I arose from my bed of pain … to a warm and solicitous welcome from our group of passengers. Ann had explained my absence from the cocktail party, and to my surprise nobody seemed to resent me being such a useless escort, and demand compensation. The passengers took me to their hearts, and before I could ask how *they* were, always asked how *I* was.

Coincidentally, the day that I arose from my sick bed was also my birthday. Unfamiliar with the shipboard birthday ritual, I was initially horrified when at dinner I was descended upon by musicians, singing waiters, and a cake; plus the cheering and applauding of the other passengers. Was this an ironic … 'at last you are with us?' Would it happen every time I was seasick?

On that first trip, I was of limited use for another reason. I remember watching someone approach our duty desk and thinking, 'whatever it is that you are going to ask – if you don't know the answer – I won't know the answer either.'

I assumed, understandably, but in the event wrongly, that Ann would be writing a long and detailed report on my presentation and general conduct, and upon this would depend my future prospects. It was paramount that I at least try to offset my disastrous start and make a good impression. What is most likely to appeal to anyone I figured, is someone who shares your own interests and style. Well too late to match Ann's array of evening shoes and multi coloured outfits with my solitary black patents and equally solitary black skirt. But whatever she proposed to do, I would do it too – enthusiastically.

Unfortunately, what Ann liked to do after a hard day's problem solving, and she was very good at the job, was to stay up till three or four in the morning drinking large amounts of alcohol. This was not against the rules, some, though very few, of our passengers stayed up late too, so technically she was socialising, and she was also good at this. My fellow trainee too, seemed to manage it. I on the other hand, eyelids drooping with fatigue at eleven thirty, would eventually beg to be allowed to go to bed. I couldn't risk pleading a headache or any other ailments as my boxes in that area were not only ticked, but completely blocked in, already.

"Oh come on," she would say brightly, "don't be a spoil sport."

Nobody is going to report favourably on a spoil sport so I tried hard to make the effort. Then there was the alcohol. I like alcohol in reasonable amounts. In large amounts alcohol does not like me. Round followed round.

"No you don't want mineral water – here have this double gin."

More rounds ... I quickly spent my meagre earnings without leaving the bar. Sometimes passengers bought us drinks too, sometimes other staff. Ann never showed any signs of intoxication, and she was also able to spring cheerfully and energetically out of bed at 8am next morning, seemingly unaffected. I figured that perhaps this was what you were expected to do – could I take it?

I also picked up from Ann that you should join in everything. Our job on this ship at least, was to help the entertainment staff to get a good atmosphere going. People liked to see us out there, particularly making fools of ourselves. I should at least be good at that. We joined in the conga round the deck, took partners for the limbo competition, bounced up and down in the aquatic bounce up and down sessions, line danced, went on excursions. If my friends, lifting their eyes from their Gabriel Garcia Márquez, could see me now, what would they think?

A lot of dancing goes on aboard ships, much more than on land, and we were expected to help out getting people onto the floor. Oh, that's another thing ... I can't dance. Well not with someone holding me and expecting me to do backwards what he is doing forwards – I just can't do it, I don't know why. I've even availed myself of the on-board dance classes, and still can't do it. So when one of the entertainment staff came purposefully across the empty dance floor towards me, in the packed entertainment lounge – I froze.

"I can't dance," I whined.

"We need to lead off – get things going."

"You'll be sorry, I warn you."

"You'll be fine," he said, taking me in a vice like grip; he was an ex dancing instructor. I wasn't fine and neither was he. He never asked me again.

Male dance hosts often mistook me for someone to dance with but were more easily disabused of their error. Male dance hosts! You tried not to think of the history of female dance hosts.

Strangely, on another ship, the adorable gay cruise director, who looked like a cross between Julian Clary and a Barbie doll, insisted on dancing with me despite my protests. We danced like Fred Astaire and Ginger Rogers – yes, me as well – I don't know how to account for that.

After the cruise I went home and waited for the fateful – 'don't ring us'. It didn't come. No-one said anything, and the passenger list duly arrived for the trip round the Baltic. I could hardly believe my luck. I armed myself with anti-seasickness wrist bands, and a full range of seasickness tablets and sallied forth. Incidentally, the wrist bands worked like magic – until one day they didn't – without the faith, they never worked again.

The ship this time was an old Russian vessel with an all Russian crew. Again I had an experienced mentor, but she couldn't have been more different. She worked hard during the days, again she did the job very well, but she spent most evenings reading in her cabin, retired early, and rose early for exercise classes. She drank very little and did not feel obliged to limbo or play bingo. The thing is, nobody actually told you how to do the job exactly, a bit like the teacher training I suppose, but in this case with more justification. As long as problems were smoothed out, head office kept informed, paperwork completed, cash floats and expenses balanced, and as long as most importantly, the passengers were happy with you – that was OK.

This latter was always a sore point with me. It wasn't good enough for passengers to say on their questionnaires that you did a good job, or even a very good job, or even for half to say that you were excellent. You were expected to get an average only just short of excellent. It was almost impossible without cheating, but I wasn't going to stoop to that. I remember, because of some cancellation compensation, having only six passengers once. Naturally I could devote a lot of time to them – give detailed timings for solo shore trips, currency conversion, I did everything but wipe their bottoms. At the end one couple – a third of my passengers remember, said,

"You've been wonderful – couldn't fault you, but we're both teachers, we never give full marks on principle." At a stroke – a lousy average.

Back to the Russian vessel. I was relieved to discover that there was more than one way to do this job, and by dint of the enclosed nature of the Baltic and the many stops, I managed to remain blissfully un-seasick.

This ship, no longer cruising, was on the idiosyncratic side. The Russian staff unlike the charming Philippino staff that I had encountered before, could be a touch surly. Standing glass in hand at the welcome party I had been alarmingly instructed to,

"Get out of my way," by a scary looking passing waitress. I tried to put it down to unfamiliarity with the language, and our very English tendency to have said – 'Oh, do excuse me, so sorry to disturb you, would you mind terribly, if I just … squeezed past.'

The food too, unlike that on other ships was not over abundant. I felt an air of, 'You've got meat and three veg – lucky you, what have you to complain about?' Matters were not helped when the chef was apparently called ashore for a funeral. I can still picture the frantic rugby type scrum around the lunch buffet one day, parting to reveal a few shreds of lettuce scattered about. Shortage of food was something I never saw again on a ship.

This was also my first introduction to dining at the captain's table. It turned out to be not typical. Twenty or so guests including me were invited to dine in the captain's private dining room. It was funny how on some ships I was an important person, hobnobbing with the officers, and on others I was somewhere below the drain un-blockers on the scale of social elevation.

Added to the anticipation on this occasion was the fact that this particular captain did not socialise, in fact he was rarely seen. I always think it's a strange job, being the captain of a cruise ship. Clearly you needed to know all about navigation etc. and how to dock – it never failed to amaze me or send a nervous shiver down my spine to see huge ships slide sideways in and out of berths. But also you needed, in the case of cruise ships, to like people, or at least pretend that you did. You needed to be sociable, and able to make witty and interesting speeches to audiences of hundreds or even thousands. Some were great at it, almost professional level entertainers, while other poor sods crept into the spotlight, stumbled through the minimum amount of:

"We have forty three nationalities working on this ship … and we are all one big happy family … and now let's welcome our second chef, Manuel Gonzales, from Portugal," and, "On this cruise you have eaten five hundred tons of steak, and three thousand gallons of ice cream …" before retreating sweating into the wings.

We were waiting outside the captain's dining room at the appointed time. Where was he? The cruise director breezed purposefully up. A cruise director is in charge of all the entertainment side of shipboard life.

"In we go," he said brightly, "captain may be a bit late."

Once seated and with 'large' small glasses filled with vodka, he rose –

"To our great ship!" he said, knocking the vodka back in one. Some passengers followed his example; the rest of us began sipping, or looking at each other.

"I don't like vodka," whispered the woman on my left. A large, small glass of neat vodka was not something I fancied either. The cruise director was brooking no nonsense.

"Drink it – like this," he said, downing another. "It would be an insult to this fine ship if you do not." He was clearly not going to have any wimpy messing about. We dutifully downed our vodka. He rose again.

"To Russia!" He pronounced this time. A tad more relaxed, we downed our vodka. He was on his feet again.

"The Queen!" Well we couldn't insult our own queen, now could we? I lost count of the number of toasts, and the captain never did turn up to his own table, perhaps he was toasting in his cabin, but we all had a good time ... I think.

I had also learned a useful lesson about ingenuity in the face of difficulty, from the cruise director.

I learned about another thing on this cruise too. How to, or not to, deal with an emergency. This although I didn't know it, was to be the first of many.

One of the things we were expected to do was to help out on the ship's excursions if we were needed. Something I was only too happy to do. On some ships they did not want your help, and it was a perk for the ship's hairdressers or shop staff, but the tour manager on this ship valued our experience. Also as most of the rest of the crew had been to these ports a dozen times, they were happy to leave it to someone else. Indeed there was a bit of a shortage of hands.

"How can I not let you go to the Kirov ballet?" asked the tour manager, "when you have been such a help, going on all those other excursions?" It was another of those – 'I never got used to

161

them' – bizarre conversations. What I remembered about the Kirov ballet was not really the dancing, but the people from the audience going up on stage after the performance to hand over bunches of flowers wrapped in newspaper, and clearly from their gardens. Imagine that at our precious Covent Garden.

If you are going to fall ill or have an accident, obviously some places are better for it to happen than others. I remember a passenger who had had a heart attack but was alert enough to see that he was lucky to be heading for the hospital in nice, Dutch, Aruba, and not Columbia in South America, which we had just left. Given the aforementioned, St. Petersburg would probably not come top of anyone's list of places in which to fall ill.

It was a coach trip to the Summer Palace. The form was that you helped the local guide. Usually you took your place at the back of the line, keeping stragglers from getting detached from the group, while the guide led at the front. This of course meant that you never heard what the guide had to say as you always caught up just as they were finishing. It sounded an easy task but was often a nightmare. Anyway, this was not the problem here. We had assembled in the foyer of the Summer Palace and were just about to set off on our tour, when a frisson of alarm ran through the crowd ... someone had been taken ill. The guide and I pushed our way to the front of the gathered passengers. A man was lying spread-eagled on the floor. We made him and his naturally anxious wife, as comfortable as we could. The guide rang for medical assistance and we all waited. Assistance came remarkably quickly, and the medical team attempted to plug him in to some monitoring equipment they had brought. None of the plugs in the entrance hall worked. In the end we had to drag the poor man behind the cloakroom counter to be within reach of the sole working socket. The medical team spoke no English but through our guide said that he should be taken to hospital. The man was adamant – he did not want to go to hospital – his wife was equally insistent. They wanted to see the ship's doctor – on the ship. You couldn't blame them. Would there be working sockets at the hospital you had to ask? Plugs definitely worked on the ship. There was a stand-off. Meanwhile several more tour groups had arrived and were milling around. It was getting crowded, and representatives from our group were beginning to mutter the dreaded:

"We've paid for this tour and ..." I could understand it, perhaps it would be their only chance to see the Summer Palace, but nevertheless, this unhappily far from solitary example of man's inhumanity to man, always depressed me. We had to do something – these were my passengers – the guide looked to me.

"I'll go back to the ship with the ambulance, and you carry on with the tour," I said, surprising myself with my 'you are always so calm' voice.

As well as the obvious: driver, doctor, nurse, none of whom spoke English, and the fact that I had taken a medical decision – what if he died? Would it be my fault? Could I be sued? There was another problem that I was only too aware of. We had each been given a permit to be in the country, with the stricture – on no account ever let this out of your possession. Mine was at this moment on the tour bus. If the patient was going to die, I didn't want it to be while I was searching among the dozens of tour buses which would be locked up anyway.

The trouble was that I had decided that, to be on the safe side, I should bring with me on this excursion my very weighty staff manual and a mass of other instructional papers, just in case I needed to check what to do in an emergency. Well as fate had revealed, in an emergency you have no time to cross reference advice from your manual, and check all your procedural updates. Because of the great weight of my briefcase I had left it on the coach with my permit. Oh dear, I'd just have to worry about that when I got back to the ship.

The Summer Palace is about an hour's drive from the dock. If that poor man had not been ill when he was put into the ambulance, he certainly would have been by the time he got out. I will swear that that ambulance had solid tyres, and the roads were horrendous, the surface cracked and broken. Despite several stomach lurching swerves to avoid them, we fell into many huge potholes. The Russian doctor directed several remarks in the direction of the patient, his quivering wife, and my quivering self. He might have been saying:

"Cold for the time of year," or, "Sadly, he is dead now," we had no idea.

Upon entering the city the comments clearly became questions – we could tell that. After a few back-trackings, and reversings, I realised that they couldn't find the dock, or the ship ... whichever – we were clearly lost. My attempt to comfort myself with the thought that, providing he lived of course, there would be Brownie points for me, was dashed when I discovered they weren't even my passengers.

After what seemed an eternity we arrived at the ship, well the barrage of custom check points through which you got to the ship. The stretcher patient and his wife were whisked through – but me – I had no pass.

"Not possible to go through."

We must have been wandering lost around St. Petersburg for a long time because shortly after this the tour bus arrived back. Some dear person had remembered to bring my briefcase. I walked up the ship's gangway, on rubbery legs.

At lunch at the staff table, white with stress, I relayed what had happened. There was a murmur of sympathy, and then the conversation turned to other things. I suddenly realised that this was no big deal. This was what the job was about, and that this or something very like it was going to happen again and again and again.

And the man? While I was at my duty desk next day, a couple appeared in front of me, smiling. They didn't register – not unusual, I often didn't recognise my own passengers.

"This is for you," they said, holding out a gift wrapped package, "for your help ... it turned out to be a false alarm ... feeling much better now." I looked again. Stripped of their anxiety and pain, I hadn't recognised them. I am looking at the jug they had bought me in Finland as I write.

Chapter Twenty

My next trip was my first unaccompanied. I had about a hundred and thirty passengers to cope with alone. Spectres of the previous two cruises, I tried to push to the back of my mind. I was getting the hang of it now. When people approached, I was fairly confident that I would be able to help.

Despite the fact that some passengers viewed me as being the lucky beneficiary of a free holiday, it was hard work, and although only a small proportion of the passengers needed my assistance, even a small proportion was still quite a lot. But I actually enjoyed it. It was satisfying sorting out people's problems, and feeling that you were helping them to enjoy their holiday. Also in those early days people only came to you with real problems, and on the whole were reasonably ... well ... reasonable.

I want to emphasise here that the vast majority of the people that I met over the twelve years that I did this job were nice, often lovely, people who I remember fondly. Well that's not strictly true, the sad fact is that you don't tend to remember nearly so clearly the nice people that behaved sensibly, and whose company and conversation you enjoyed. There were hundreds and hundreds of them who were charming and interesting, and a pleasure to meet, but you tend to remember instead the people who haunt your dreams with their awfulness. I won't name any names; I couldn't if I wanted to. It was hard enough learning the names and faces at the time, but however vivid they loomed during the cruise, names were immediately forgotten when I got home. But you know who you are!

Over the years people seemed to become a lot more 'demanding' and not in a good way.

There were the two women – whenever I saw them I thought of he ugly sisters in Cinderella. It wasn't their faces, it was their unremitting nastiness. With great difficulty I had solved one of their numerous complaints and had secured a table for them on the second sitting at dinner. I rushed to intercept them on their way to the despised first sitting.

"I've got you a table on second sitting," I panted, smiling. At which point they pinned me against the wall and snarled,

"Well that's what you're here for, isn't it? And what are you doing telling us now, when we are dressed and ready for first sitting tonight?"

Then there were the group of three travelling together. They fancied that they were a bit on the aristocratic side, and I was of course just an inferior pleb. One of them, disgusted already with the service she had perceived that she had been offered, had withdrawn her patronage from my company, and was travelling independently, but still expected me to help her. On a flight to New York, and before I realised that although her friends were in my group, she wasn't; she asked me how long it would take her to walk from her hotel to the Metropolitan Museum, and what time it opened? Although I didn't know this particular hotel, I knew its street, and I knew New York quite well as it happened.

"Oh, approximately half an hour, and you can check with the hotel, but it opens at about ..."

"I don't want to know 'approximately' ... I don't want to know 'about' ... I want to know exactly ... don't you know *anything* about this city?" she screamed, to the alarm of not only me, but people sitting for several rows around. The three of them, well I'm afraid it was mainly the women kept this up for the whole trip. When I realised that I had no obligation to Lady Nightmare, I could smile sympathetically, as I heard her screaming at the poor ship's receptionist, that she demanded to be flown home immediately from this impossibly dreadful ship.

Then there was what should have been a lovely cruise. Starting from New Zealand and cruising through a mouth-watering selection of islands of the South Pacific, then flying back from Tahiti. I could see trouble coming from one direction before we started. By this time we were phoning passengers before departure to introduce ourselves. This was usually appreciated, and rather nice, since people felt they knew you when you met. I would make notes on the passenger list – lady whose cat was sleeping in her case, or very frequently – SN – for sounds nice.

This man sounded grumpy and angry even at this early stage. This was a dream holiday – lighten up! Then he mentioned that he was staying pre-cruise at, 'The Auckland Hotel'. Well I knew Auckland a bit too. I checked – I was right, there was no 'Auckland Hotel'. As he was arriving two days early in order to meet a relative at the said hotel, I thought I'd better warn him, and we could establish where he was really staying. He was incandescent with rage. I received a call from my supervisor. What was I doing upsetting the passengers? It turned out that he had asked for a couple of extra nights at the tour hotel, and had been informed that two extra nights had been booked for him at the Auckland hotel. Both he and his wife notched up literally dozens of complaints. But I was so proud, when he marched sullenly into our cocktail party, and growled; no he didn't want champagne or any of that other rubbish – he wanted beer, and it had to be – he named a particular brand. By some amazing coincidence we had it!

It never rains but it pours, amazingly he was not the worst person on that trip. Amazing, because it was only a small group. The phone rang at 5am in my room in the 'Auckland Hotel'. A man reported that his wife was haemorrhaging and he was taking her to hospital. My heart sank – poor man – poor woman, after coming all this way. As often happens I needed to be in two places at the same time. If they needed to be left behind, there was a rep in Auckland who would look after them, it was just the, would they, wouldn't they, make it. I sent the other passengers off to the

168

ship and waited with the unfortunate couple's luggage. At the eleventh hour I got the call. If the ship's doctor was happy with the hospital diagnosis she could go. Taxi to the ship with the luggage. Tense wait while the doctor studied the report – yes they could sail. I gave her a big hug.

"I'm so pleased for you, you must be so relieved."

"Wasn't bothered," she shrugged. Afterwards I discovered that the hospital's report concluded – 'heavy period'.

My delight at her, 'making it' quickly evaporated. Nothing was right ... ever. This unsatisfactory state of affairs culminated at my desk one day.

"I want to go home," she said. I enquired as to the reason for this wish.

"I'm not enjoying it – in fact I'm fed up." Bit flimsy for repatriation.

"Anything ... else?" I asked, keeping steely self-control.

"... and I'm constipated."

I explained in as level a tone as I could muster, that summoning the air ambulance for private repatriation from the South Pacific, for someone who was a bit fed up and constipated would not go down too well with the insurance company.

It didn't help either, that we had to take frequent diversionary action to avoid a tropical hurricane in the area. We had to miss out our first port of call, but were promised Fiji instead. Then just as we were approaching Fiji – looking gorgeous – we were told that we couldn't stop there because although it looked idyllic now, the storm was due there in a few hours. It was disappointing but alternatives were worked out, and we did see the damage that had been inflicted. All this presented me with a slightly surreal task when writing the reports that needed to accompany every 'happening' while at the same time crossing the International date line. 'On the first 23rd March, we had to abandon plans to ...' 'On the second 23rd March we ...' It did give me two birthdays though, but I don't remember getting two lots of singing waiters, or cakes.

Mr and Mrs, 'I want to go home'(funnily enough she always

seemed to be having a good time when she didn't know I was watching) had one last fling, just when I thought I was literally home and dry. We were flying into Paris to change planes. Our flight was late, and we had a tight connection time. I moved down the plane warning passengers that we would have to move fast. They were near the back.

"We're not hurrying," said Mr Awkward.

I consulted with the stewardess. There were a couple of empty seats near the front. We could move them there; it would give them a slight advantage.

"We're not moving ... my wife's asleep, and I'm not waking her."

"Well, if she wakes up ..."

"We're not moving."

"OK, well in that case I can't guarantee that you'll catch the connecting flight, but flights are pretty frequent and you can ..."

"It's your job to get us on that flight."

I sometimes muse as to how some of these people hold down jobs, families and ... surely they couldn't have any friends. I did manage one parting bit of advice – that they should think carefully before embarking on any more far flung (or even near flung) holidays, due to his wife's ... delicacy. I enjoyed that.

I was worried in advance about the cruise from Venice. For some reason we were flying into Milan, and there was only just enough time to make the connection by coach. "What if the plane was delayed?" I asked.

"Oh, just fix up accommodation for the passengers, and then fly them on to meet the ship the next day." What? Find hotel rooms for forty odd passengers in Venice at a couple of hours notice and then flights at equally no notice – I didn't like the sound of that.

Needless to say, the flight was delayed, and I found myself in Milan with a wheelchair and a couple of passengers missing, and the coach driver saying that we had to leave right now, or he wouldn't be responsible if we missed the sail time. The wheelchair turned up, the passengers turned up. I heaved a sigh of relief, and we all boarded the coach.

"Excuse me," a passenger tapped me on the shoulder, "I am taking diuretic tablets, we will have to make a toilet stop ... perhaps two."

"I really don't think ..." I began.

"We have to," he said firmly.

I consulted with the driver and guide. We were really late and they would not be held responsible if we missed the ship. Ships don't wait. I knew that from past experience. I also knew from past experience that if we made a toilet stop, everyone would suddenly want to go – long queues in the ladies – no.

"I'm so sorry but we really can't," I said firmly. "I can't risk everyone else missing the sailing in order for us to stop for you." Surely he would understand.

"I don't care if everyone else misses the sailing because of me," was his reply. I furtively kept an eye on his crotch, but we didn't stop. Just as well, as when we arrived in Venice the coach driver couldn't find the dock. We could all see the ship, and pointed and shouted in unison like some pantomime audience:

"It's over there!" "It's behind you!"

We arrived with ten minutes to get through customs and on board. The ship sailed two hours late.

This was a cruise whose theme – unintentional – was ... fires on board. Passengers are often asked at safety meetings,

"What is the biggest danger on board a ship?" The hoped for replies are: collision, sinking, falling overboard, overeating ... etc. So that, 'fire' can be produced – well not literally, except in this case, with a flourish.

I know that you never really expect these things to happen. So when I heard the seven blasts on the ship's whistle at 1am, I couldn't really believe it. It was a practice surely – at 1am though?

I opened the cabin door – the corridor was full of smoke. Funny how you absorb things you think you haven't absorbed: put on sweater, leave everything behind, go straight to muster station.

Any cruisers will recognise that on arrival, when you are tired, wanting to look round, or relax, this muster practise is what you have to do. Here was the proof that it was not just an annoyance but a necessity.

We all mustered on deck, donned our life jackets, and waited. There was no doubt that the ship was on fire. Clouds of black smoke billowed from the stern into the night sky. It just so happened that there were a lot of Italian honeymoon couples on board. I don't know if it was the prospect of having the dream life they had planned, snatched away from them, but there was much loud crying. The older passengers, with stiff upper lips, and comments about living through the war, were brilliant. I looked at the billowing smoke. It was getting worse. I looked at the black water – we'd be in there soon. I saw no lifeboats being lowered. I mentally rehearsed the 'arm across chest, hold nose' jumping in instructions.

Just in time, I gathered afterwards, they got it under control. Someone had thrown a lighted cigarette end over the side, and the wind had blown it back into a rope locker on a lower deck. People were always doing this, clearly with no idea of the possible consequences.

Amazingly, as these are the only two fires I have ever seen at sea, days later we stood by, ready to take evacuees as another ship battled with a fire in its kitchen. We missed a day's itinerary there, but there were no complaints. A fire on a ship, preferably another ship, was quite interesting to watch … from a ship that wasn't on fire.

Excursions, were always a source of danger. I ended up quite happily letting some other eager, wide eyed … mug, do it. Things, 'happened' on excursions, as I had already discovered. Lunch was often enlivened by tales of accidents, lost passengers, lost handbags, etc. Although you weren't actually on your own on excursions, there were only two of you. The taxi trip back to the ship with the passenger who had fainted, tripped, fallen, became quite familiar. I could try to make sure that I had local currency, but the local language was not so easy. After the St. Petersburg incident, I now always carried a picture postcard of the ship, and the ship's programme with the name of the dock on it. One passenger I would have liked to get into a taxi was the one who had developed acute diarrhoea, of the every five minute variety, but who insisted on getting on the coach for the hours return journey. Then there was that time in Monaco, when getting off the coach, parked in a vast underground car park, a young woman asked if her gran should bring her oxygen cylinder.

"Well do you think she will need it?"

"Oh yes."

"Well, better get it then," I replied, through clenched teeth. By the time we had the oxygen cylinder we could just catch the tail end of the disappearing crocodile if we ran. 'Can't run.' No, of course she couldn't, and she couldn't walk far either. How we made it out of the car park into the town, and joined up with the rest of the group I don't know.

People were always booking to do things that they couldn't do. However many warnings they got about the fifty steps, the cobbled road, the 'lot of walking' there were always the few people who had booked an excursion that they were incapable of doing. However often you asked guides to slow down for the people hobbling along at a snail's pace at the back they didn't. I could see both sides of it. The guide had to get through the itinerary and back to the ship before lunch, or sailing time. People really wanted to see The Hermitage, or the Antarctic, or even the centre of Monaco, but they were not capable of doing it, and just chose to ignore this fact and hope that some miracle would carry them through.

Ah yes, I remember this particular Monaco excursion for something else too. When we got back to the coach, a couple had taken another couple's seat at the front for the return journey – they refused to move. Front seats are so important aren't they?! People would arrive an hour early to be sure to get one. The 'injured parties' angrily declared that they were not going to sit anywhere other than in those seats. There was a stand-off, and very nearly a punch up. I took the standing couple aside.

"It's only a seat," I soothed ... "if they are so childish, perhaps you ... moral high ground ... more mature."

The main and constantly recurring problem though, was finding the last few passengers after a stop, and getting them back on the coach. If you recognise yourself here, hang your head, take note, and amend your ways. Part of the excursion escort's job was to check at all times that everyone was accounted for before the coach set off after a stop. Ninety five percent of people were back at the given time – always; and there were always, but always, those few who were nowhere in sight. Apart from the few who just couldn't remember what time they had been given for return to the bus, and were on their way to remembering nothing at all – the general attitude of the others was, 'Oh they'll wait, they won't go without us.' The fact that everyone else had made the effort, and were now sitting wasting time waiting for them didn't seem to bother them one jot. They were usually to be found at the end of some long queue for ice cream, or choosing postcards, or just settling down at a table with a cup of coffee. I would really have liked to leave them at the North Cape, or the village in the mountains, but you couldn't. My favourite, guide's tactic, delivered with beguiling sweetness was:

"If you are not here by half past, I will assume that you have chosen to make your own way back to the ship." Wow! How that worked.

I have to admit here, that years later on organised trips myself, I often walked away from the coach and then an hour later was thinking – 'what time did the guide say? Where did he say the coach was going to be?' I discovered that a kind of, 'mind switch off' seems to occur on coaches.

People, for one reason or another, did sometimes get left behind. Perhaps some escorts did not count them five times like me. I remember one man – he and his wife were on an excursion to Santiago de Compostela. Coaches aren't allowed into the town and parked a couple of hundred yards away. When the time came to leave, his wife who had opted for a cup of coffee instead of a last walk around, was there, but he was not. The guide and escort looked for him, but he couldn't be found. The ship was sailing shortly, people wanted their lunch, the coach had to go. He was one of our group. I was working with someone else on this ship – we were no longer expected to manage a hundred and fifty passengers on our own. The minutes ticked by – half an hour to sailing. Should one of us pack a bag, and stay on shore? His wife was upset, but not, I noticed, inconsolable. With minutes to spare, he arrived back in a taxi. A member of the ship's staff ran out to pay the fare. Was he humble? Was he apologetic? Not a bit of it. It turned out that it wasn't his fault at all – it was his wife's fault for not keeping an eye on him – the guide's fault for not waiting – but most of all, the fault of all those stupid foreigners, who didn't understand his demands for directions – they couldn't even speak English!

I do remember the ship going back for someone – just once. I remember the guy appearing on the deserted dock when we were a hundred yards or so out to sea. What a forlorn figure he looked. Watching the ship leave port was a popular pastime, so there were plenty of people to witness this interesting development. A lifeboat was lowered and went to pick him up. Large crowds had gathered along the rails by now. There was no gangway of course, so hundreds of us saw him quite well enough to recognise him again, as he climbed up the rope ladder, and was bundled unceremoniously through a hole in the ships side.

Probably the worst thing about excursions was that people complained about them so much. Occasionally there was a justifiable complaint but mainly it was just that what they saw did not measure up to their often totally unrealistic expectations. I can remember on one of my own holidays, arriving for the first time in Yugoslavia, in March, to be greeted by pouring, chilly rain, not at all what I had envisaged, which was some sort of exotic, tropical, palm-tree paradise. At least I could see that this was my own fault. Such self awareness was pretty rare among excursion passengers.

A thousand times I pointed out that sorry though I was that they had been disappointed with what they had seen, the tour can only show you what is there. I despaired – that scene in Fawlty Towers summed it up – did they expect to see herds of wildebeest sweeping majestically across the plain, in Minorca, or the hanging gardens of Babylon on the Costa del Sol?

There was that group of travel agents, who for goodness sake, should have known better, who complained bitterly about a tour along the Douro valley in Portugal.

"Waste of money," they grumbled angrily "it looked just like ... England."

I remember them too, because one of them mistakenly took my case from the quay on our return to Southampton. Wait, I was advised, people always realise pretty quickly and will come back with it. Not when they've put it in the boot of their car and gone straight to work they don't.

Then there was the equally disgusted lady who said of Tangier,

"... But it's so dirty, you'd think someone would have cleaned it up before we came."

I remember too the man who booked a walking tour of Tallin.

"First," began the guide when we got off the coach, "we are going to walk to ..."

"What? We have to walk?... I'm not walking ..."

My all time favourite comment though, was on a ship cruising up the east coast of America. A shuttle bus had been organised to take passengers from the dock, to the nearest town. A lady stopped at my desk.

"Where do I catch this shuttle bus?" she drawled.

"Well if you follow the arrows along this corridor, and up the stairs, the gangway is ... "

"Oh no! I have to go to the ... gangway?"

I explained with commendable gravity, I thought, that unfortunately that was the case, as they found it so difficult to get the buses on board the ship. She didn't bat an eyelid. She didn't get it.

I had heard about a lady asking at the tour desk, if the horse riding being offered, was going to be on shore or on the ship. I didn't believe it then; I believed it now.

Why people did complain so much about excursions I'm not sure, as within ten minutes of leaving the quay, most people, including often I'm afraid me, were asleep. Well it was usually an early start, or after lunch, and there was something so soothing about the engine noise, the gentle rocking motion, and the guides voice telling you that the fine town hall on the left had been built in 1897, and to note the intricate carving around the window which had been designed by …

I remember one excursion when the guide facing a sea of drooping eyelids and gaping mouths, had said that on the return journey he would not disturb our slumber, and would keep quiet. Do you know – insomnia struck – none of us could drop off at all.

Everyone else was allowed to fall asleep, but really I shouldn't – it was a problem.

On one river trip, my partner and I were responsible for doing everything: on board entertainment, excursions, organising the coaches, collecting the cash, the lot. I was so worn out that I fell asleep on every excursion coach. I sat at the back next to the same couple every day. She sat in the window seat, then her husband, then me. In the end I used to say,

"I'm coming to sleep with your husband again."

I was always desperate to get on an Alaska trip – but it eluded me; it was covered by American or Canadian escorts, or you needed to commit to six months. Then one day my luck was in – I got one. As you might guess, I spent a long time deciding how many heavy sweaters as oppose to light sweaters, I was going to need. Taxi to coach, coach to Heathrow. Phoned my husband.

"Trip's been cancelled," he said. Oh yeah? – we like to pull each other's leg. Then I was met by a man who said he was from the shipping company.

"Sorry trip has been cancelled, engine trouble, I tried to get you at home but couldn't."

Chapter Twenty-one

Of all the things that I saw while doing this job, the most amazing has to be the one at the other end of the planet to Alaska – the Antarctic.

Needless to say there was the, what to take, dilemma. Would you need evening wear in the Antarctic? Well it was still a cruise ship. How cold was it going to be? I didn't know. But my most pressing decision and biggest mistake was the boots. I would surely need boots, but should I take the full length, heavy grip wellingtons, or the fur lined rubber boots that I had found so useful in Nova Scotia, or these huge padded moon boots. I couldn't decide and ended up doing what I often did in such circumstances, and took all three. Even more stupidly, I dragged them all back. Well the moon boots weren't mine, and I couldn't decide which of the other two to leave. Rubber boots were available as it happened, because people it seemed kept turning up expecting to go ashore in the Antarctic in their loafers.

Boots aside. The Antarctic – how beautiful – how interesting is it? It's sell your house, pawn your children, do it before you die – interesting and beautiful. Definitely try to do it before you die, or you won't get the best out of it. And don't leave it, if possible, until you are nearly ninety, have difficulty standing up, hearing, or seeing, and can't find anyone to go with you. I sympathised, and in a way, admired the two ladies (not together) who did, but you are asking for trouble, and they got it.

We sailed from Ushuia, an interesting town originally built up around a prison, on the southern-most tip of South America. A place where the phrase 'changeable weather' must have been invented. Every fifteen minutes the sun either came out, or the rain lashed down. It was cold but somehow I'd expected it to be colder; Ushuia didn't feature on the international weather tables. Gardener that I am, I marvelled on a visit to Tierra del Fuego National Park as to how they had so many plants from my own garden, down there. Mmmm ... I don't think Darwin collected plants from Warwickshire and took them to South America ... or did he?

I was doing three trips – six weeks. By this time, six weeks was beginning to seem a long time to be away from home. I had pondered this. Chewing it over with one of my sons, he had said,

"Look at it this way, when you are on your deathbed, will you think – I'm so glad I didn't go to the Antarctic, because I got the wardrobe cleared out, and painted the bathroom." Of course not. How wise was he? Or possibly how stupid was I, to even waver?

Three trips meant, tiresomely, multiple crossings of Drake's Passage. It was always rough, even in a large metal ship, and with maps and a crew who knew what they were doing. Imagine doing it in a small wooden ship, and with no maps, or charts.

It was all amazing ... really amazing. Rocky outcrops, at first, of sea-lions, and seals – skuas wheeling overhead; then the blueness, the blinding whiteness, the sun on an endless vista of glittering, untouched snow; a Leopard seal sunning himself on an ice floe. Bundled up against a horizontal snow blizzard one minute, and swimming in the 'hot' spring, bubbling up through the icy sea, the next ... the rubber zodiacs ... the penguins.

Discovery – penguins are every bit as cute as they look in pictures, but pictures don't tell you about the smell. You can smell them, way, way, before you step out among them. But they were worth it. I had a privilege the passengers didn't get. Because I was revisiting them every two weeks, I got to see the chicks grow from tiny mites peeping out from under mother's, or perhaps it was father's feathers, to strapping teenagers ready to leave home. Later we saw one whole 'gang' I suppose of teenage penguins, hanging out on the edge of an ice floe – not an adult in sight. How sensible are penguins? They leave their teenagers, and bugger off. What do the teenagers do? Hang around for a bit: smoking, getting drunk, pushing over tombstones, and annoying passers-by? Unfortunately for them, these options are not open to teenage penguins. Eventually they get so hungry and possibly bored with no adults to torment, that they literally, take the plunge and start feeding and looking after themselves. For goodness sake! If penguins could work this out, why are we still pussy footing about? It does make you worry about the theory of natural selection. Did we cheat somewhere along the line?

We visited research stations too. People were usually quite pleased to see us. I don't think that they are bothered by too many casual callers. As each station was a little outpost of that country, the various ways in which we were received was interesting.

At the American base we had a rather earnest tour of the impressive facilities, and explanation of the work that they were carrying out, with a decidedly 'we're doing a good job here' slant. I did love the brave, wind smashed, cardboard palm tree outside their little theatre though. I wonder what sort of productions they put on – South Pacific?

By contrast, the Italian base (and this was the day before they returned home for the Antarctic winter, so were packing – tell me about it!) received us with a big, 'kiss on both cheeks ... mamma mia,' type welcome. There was fresh brewed coffee, and lovely chocolate, and a lot of smiling and hugging, to warm us up.

So few ships did this run then, that there were half a dozen escorts on board from different travel companies, and we shared a table at dinner. One evening the conversation got round to the inevitable subject of pay. I was now earning a lot – well a bit more than my starting salary, but when I revealed my salary, there was stunned silence. Eventually one of them said in contradictory fashion, "I don't know what to say." It seemed that they were all earning a day, what I was earning a week, plus American level tipping. Tipping was still a no-no for me.

"Why do you do this?" asked another incredulously.

The reason that I did it was neatly and immediately revealed.

The third trip was a different one. The first two trips had been to the Antarctic peninsula – gorgeous and fascinating enough – but on the third trip instead of returning to Ushuia, we were to head south, as near as you could get to the South Pole by sea, and from there go on to New Zealand. Very few civilian, or any other ships did this.

We steamed south – fast. It was hard not to be a bit apprehensive. Huge icebergs were all around us, at least one, a mile long, and we were speeding in what seemed a straight line between them. Did icebergs form neat, straight rows? I doubted it. Perhaps I'd better have a word with the captain. I wished I didn't know about the Titanic.

There could be few more isolated places on earth – well not where people with evening wear and wellingtons go. If something happened, you couldn't just abandon ship as if you were in the Adriatic, where surely people would have noticed your ship on fire, and land and ships were all around, and the water was not freezing, and kept so by mile long ice cubes. There was nobody to see you here; no habitation of any kind, except for the couple of, packing and going home, research stations. No other ships to evacuate to, and even if your SOS was heard, what could anyone do? If anyone did come to your rescue, how long could you survive in that water? I'm no expert but I reckon about five minutes before hypothermia got you. We steamed on – fast – seeing no sign of human anything for days.

Then something bizarre happened. We passed Shackleton's hut. We couldn't stop because landing conditions were too bad. You kind of forgot that there were to be no quay-sides here, with tour buses lined up, and tables selling those essential kaftans and phallic carvings. There was no anything, and if the weather was bad, the water was choppy or the shoreline shifty, you couldn't go – that was it.

Some moments stay with you, and this was one of them. As we passed this tiny ramshackle hut in its humblingly vast and empty setting, I was in the gym, trying to shift the effects of four weeks of overeating. That particular gym was a fancy wrap-around, glass affair at the front of the ship. I stood in the warm, in my leotard, suffering from a surfeit of fancy food, and looked out on that scene, that still somehow looked haunted by hardship, suffering, and death. I've got tears in my eyes now as I write this. What a strange world we live in.

An even more humbling and tear choking experience was to come. We had the key to Scott's hut. I don't suppose passing opportunistic break-ins were a problem, but anyway, there would be no-one at home and it was locked. The chances of an ordinary mortal like me, getting to see inside Scott's hut are miniscule. For a start we were only the third passenger ship to make it so far that summer, and summer was now over, hence the research stations packing up and heading home. But even the ships that did make it this far south usually found it impossible to land a number of people safely, and heavens you couldn't just let some go and not others. If there was ever a justifiable cause for a ship's mutiny, that would be it. It was also revealed that on the two preceding years, sea conditions had made it impossible for this ship to organise a landing at Scott's hut. I could appreciate how important sea conditions were. After a previous landing on the peninsula, the wind had suddenly got up, the water became choppy, and although we returned to the ship immediately, it was both difficult and dangerous to get out of the zodiac and onto the ship's ladder with the small rubber boat rising and falling and crashing against the ship's hull.

But now, by some miracle, we were going to make it. It was a jaw dropping and humbling experience, and being an Olympic gold medal level blubberer, I could hardly bear it.

There preserved by the cold was everything ... everything ... just as they had left it, before setting out on that fateful journey: the boots hanging on the ends of the bunks, the dishes and bottles on the table, the rusted tins of food in the kitchen area, the glass test tubes and lab equipment, a newspaper dated 1908, the stables of the ill advised horses, the pile of fuel blubber outside the door, the spare skis still fastened to the outside wall. It was exactly as in the pictures you saw. Except for the dead penguin lying on its back on Scott's study table – I hoped that it had been placed there for study purposes. Even this attempt at irreverent lightweight thought could not dispel the sense of awe. I have never been in a place so weighed down with such overwhelming sadness, so poignant, so frozen, literally and metaphorically in time.

When I staggered, reeling, out through the flimsy door, a passenger offered to take a photo of me – well you couldn't say, "No, clear off, I'm traumatised,"could you? That was the hardest smile I've ever had to muster.

For scary moments, apart from our sprint through the icebergs, I think it has to be at McMurdo Research Station, our southern most point. There was no ice covering the water around us when we arrived, and set off to look round the base, but now, as we waited for the last zodiacs back, ice was thickening all around the ship. It was being rapidly and visibly overtaken by the approaching Antarctic winter. We were quite clearly being iced in. How were the researchers to get out? Well they were being transported as we watched, by helicopter to an ice breaker out in the Sound. I had heard about ships being iced in. Wasn't Shackleton iced in? There was nothing you could do but sit it out, hope your boat wasn't crushed by the pressure of the ice, that you didn't freeze or starve – would we have enough ice cream, and lobster – and wait till the arrival of the next summer. Would the captain then say in his farewell speech:

" On this trip you have eaten, 645 penguins, 237 seals, 5 deceased passengers and 300,000 gallons of ice-cream ... well, forget the cream ... just ice really."

We battled our way through the encroaching ice, and beat a hasty retreat.

When we arrived at Lyttleton near Christchurch in New Zealand, it was almost too hard to bear the sensory overload – green – bright and ... well ... green, was everywhere. I realised that I hadn't seen a speck of green, surely our national colour, for six weeks, just shades of grey and white, and a bit of blue. Here was a great sheet of blue, dotted with tiny white sailing boats, and sunny blue sky that we hadn't seen since we left the peninsula. But it was those overwhelming amounts of every shade of green imaginable that had your eyes out on stalks. And when I went walking on the shore – no boots or Arctic gear needed – there were gardens with roses, geraniums, wicket gates, window boxes. Take it easy now … slowly … digest carefully … don't overdo it to start with. I felt like someone who had come from another world, and I had.

Chapter Twenty-two

I learned such a lot in that job about all sorts of things, but mostly about people, and about myself too. I wish I could say I remembered a lot from the hundreds of museums, churches, cathedrals, tourist centres, historical reconstructions, folklore evenings, etc. that I must have seen, but truthfully I can't.

I remember the mind boggling collection of modern art at The Hermitage. The Gold Museum in Lima, before half of it was removed by 'the authorities' as fake. I remember the crouching mummies with their sewn up mouths in the Atacama desert museums, and the chocolate at the museum at St. Pierre on Martinique, that had not melted but been fossilised, by a volcanic eruption – it had happened so quickly; oh, and that the only survivor in the town was the man in jail. I remember the wonderfully ornately carved ship – The Vasa, in its Stockholm museum, and that it had sunk immediately on its maiden voyage because the design was top heavy – oops – how embarrassing for somebody. Well at least that wasn't one of my mistakes.

I suppose if I thought hard I might remember other 'worthwhile facts' but as you might have gathered 'worthwhile facts' particularly historical ones, are not really my forte.

I remember how in one small port in Newfoundland, the mayoress accompanied by her Newfoundland dog, shook hands with everyone personally as they disembarked, and the entire population turned out to welcome us, and show us around. Would this happen on our return to New York the captain mused? I remember too on that trip the amazing full eclipse of the sun, for which we were perfectly positioned at sea.

I remember I learned that you do need to take Mastercard and Visa. I learned this at the hospital in Ushuia where the passenger that the doctor and I were trying to get admitted, only had one sort and they wouldn't take it, and we didn't fancy offering ours.

But what I learned most, was a huge amount about human nature, and many, many, worthwhile lessons on how you should live your life, and for those, surely more important than which year some church was built, I am indebted to my 'teachers'.

I learned that grown up people, not just toddlers, throw tantrums, real tantrums, and that it is not a pretty sight and not to be recommended, even though as with toddlers it is often forgotten by next day. Tantrums are not something I do, which accounts for my surprise. I remember one woman who accosted me outside the ship's restaurant. Everything had been wrong in there it seemed: the food, the service, the lighting was too dim, even the chairs were too low. She yelled and stamped, while her husband stood patiently by.

"I'll go and see what I can do," I soothed – about lights being too dim, chairs too low? "Wait here I'll be back in a few minutes."

"I'm not waiting here," she screamed, and was gone.

Next morning, leaning on the ship's rail I realised that Mrs Tantrum was leaning next to me.

"Lovely morning isn't it?" she said brightly, "I just love watching the ship dock."

I am noticing that women seem to be featuring heavily in the people behaving badly category, and to be honest they often did. But they also featured heavily at the other end of the scale too. I never worried about women travelling on their own, they made friends, joined in, had fun. And I wish I had a pound for every woman who said to me something along the lines of:

"We were married for fifty years; Bert never wanted to cruise / travel / eat foreign food / mix with Johnny Foreigner. He liked, Bournemouth / Prestatyn / Skegness, so that's where we went. I'm sorry he's gone, but now I'm doing what I want to do."

Good luck to them, and men beware. I see the 'doing it before husband dies' only around the corner – what a bad example am I!

I used to have to bite my tongue on those many other occasions – I was not there to incite divorce – when an agitated woman would say,

"Have you seen Stan, I arranged to meet him here, and I can't find him?"

"Relax, he has to be around somewhere – we're at sea."

"Yes but he gets so cross if anything goes wrong and … "

Let him, I felt liked snarling.

Men on the whole though were better behaved, a tad grumpy perhaps; but men on their own were often sad and lost. I suspect their wives used to do all the social bits and pieces and they had had no practice. Despite my nudging or encouraging them, they often hung about alone, or worse still attached themselves to me. I really couldn't spend too much time with anyone – the passengers didn't like it. Once I gave in to my table companions' invitations to join them watching the show. They were shocked when one of my passengers ploughed her way through the audience to me, tapped me on the shoulder and said, pointedly,

"Sorry to disturb you when you are with your … friends."

I remember one desperately sad case where a man had embarked upon a particular cruise because his late wife had always wanted to do it. Of course everything made him sadder and sadder. I couldn't help feeling that she must be looking down and saying,

"Oh John, for goodness sake – what a ridiculous idea."

I learned that people have totally unrealistic ideas about life on board. Often people turned up on board who should never have been there. Sometimes you had to suspect that the family was behind it. After all a ship was a safe place wasn't it? You couldn't get lost, could you? 'They' would look after your elderly relative, and you would get two weeks off. Actually a ship is not an easy place to be. Even using lifts, there is a lot of walking. The decks and endless corridors of cabin doors can be confusing. Heavens, I've had nightmares – real ones – about wandering down endless corridors looking for my cabin. Sometimes in these dreams I had remembered my cabin number, and sometimes no-one could help me because I had not.

Whose idea was it then to send a totally blind man on a cruise on his own? The poor man was weeping by day two and begging to be sent home. He wasn't in my group, but we all took it in turns to look after him.

People in the first and even second stages of dementia turn up; 'Oh, everyone will look out for them.' I assume they are sent by family, because often they are way past being able to book for themselves. It's not so easy. There is a lot to take in and deal with. On occasion I've not noticed the time change on the daily programme and have wondered where everyone is at 6am. You really need to have your wits about you. I remember one lady I endlessly checked on, and chased, to make sure she knew what she was doing and got to where she should be at the right time. As we parted on the quay she looked at my jacket and said,

"Oh, do you work for this company then?"

Another poor lady wandered into the show lounge one evening – the compère was in the middle of a joke:

"… So … there is this baby crying in a cabin …"

"Is there?" she said, joining him in the spotlight on stage. "Would you like me to go and check?" There followed a ten minute double act, of which she fortunately was totally unaware. You didn't know whether to laugh or cry.

I learned too that everyone else's job seems easier than yours, but that other people make mistakes too, and you need to try to be forgiving. I once spent half an hour dashing around Kennedy airport, while passengers waited in the coach outside, looking for two missing people. They were on my passenger list and the airline official at Heathrow had assured me that they had checked in. I hadn't been able to find them on the plane. Could they have spent the whole flight in the toilets? Eventually I gave up.

"I've got a problem," I admitted to the receptionist when we finally arrived at the hotel, "Mr and Mrs Smith seem to have disappeared into thin air."

"Oh, they cancelled two days ago," said the receptionist airily, "didn't anyone tell you?"

Then there was the time when out of the blue, a ticket and passenger list plopped onto my doormat one Bank Holiday Saturday, to sail to New York on ... Monday! I knew nothing about this. The office was of course closed. With enormous difficulty I found the phone number of my supervisor.

"Oops," she said, "did I forget to tell you? ... Sorry." And she was someone that I loved dearly ... really. But enough of other peoples mistakes; I have enough of my own.

I did that New York run as often as I could, because my son and daughter-in-law lived ten minutes walk ... walk mind ... from the ship's berth in Manhattan. How common could it be to set foot in North America, and be ten minutes walk from your destination?

You also got the added interest on transatlantic runs, of celebrities. How often do you get to rub shoulders with Rachel Hunter in the gym, or nod to Rod Stewart jogging round the deck, or share a desk with Terence Stamp? I had managed on other cruises to get Peter Hilary to our cocktail party, and a contingent from the Archers to another, but the QE2 was the best stamping ground for celebrities. Although I would swear that I am not interested in 'celebrities', when they are actually there, it's hard not to be just a teeny bit interested. Forgive me for name dropping. I have so few to drop.

Sometimes I didn't even recognise that it was an 'important' person that I was dealing with. I once got an invitation to a birthday party. I couldn't find any record of the cabin number I'd been given. Was it some converted broom cupboard that had never even made it onto the plan? No it was the split level penthouse with its own deck and butler. I'm so glad I didn't take that lipstick or talc for a gift, and opted, in a cowardly way, for no gift. The birthday girl turned out to be a lady who controlled one of the biggest cosmetic firms in the world – and very nice she was too. I do have some vague but worrying memories that I actually gave her some advice on dealing with the advent of your fiftieth birthday – like I would know, and she wouldn't!

I learned something else on that run. You know how you always take more clothes than you need and bring half of them back unworn and wonder why you took them in the first place? Well here's why. It was a five day trip; I got to know exactly what I needed – so why was I dragging along all that other, 'in case' stuff? One trip I didn't. That was the trip that I put the too hot iron on the back of my little silky top in the laundry room, and left a large iron shaped hole with crispy, stand up edges. What was I to do? I hadn't got another, and I was invited that evening to the officers' party. I put my thin (see through?) evening jacket over it, and hoped that I wouldn't forget and take it off … or that someone wouldn't put a hand on my back to guide me forward to introduce me to someone.

Then walking round the deck one breezy day in my navy silk jacket, white paint from a crew member's brush splattered over me, and couldn't be removed. Sartorial accidents like this had never happened before, and never happened again – when of course I had reverted to taking everything but the kitchen sink.

I was actually rather good at choosing from this now admittedly vast wardrobe. Well it contained everything, didn't it? I usually had an umbrella when that downpour hit. I could usually strip to something decent when the sun unexpectedly came out. Satisfyingly people often said – "Ruth always gets the clothes right." Perhaps that was why that lady phoned my cabin at 4.45am to ask if I thought that she needed a cardigan for today's excursion. To balance things up gender-wise, there was the man who phoned at about the same hour one day to remind me that it was his birthday – I knew.

Actually it was my husband who fielded that call. He accompanied me for one trip – just the one. Well it was a particularly disaster prone one. The one where the shipping company had double booked some of the cabins, so that when the second plane load of passengers arrived in Barbados, other people had already settled into their cabins, and there was nowhere for them to go. Then there was a muddle about arrangements for return journeys. Some people didn't seem to have any, and some were wrong. I think they must have been worked out, or not, at the office Christmas party. Of course as it was Christmas no-one was in the office to answer questions about the time of the train to Chelmsford. Should I ring the emergency number? I didn't think the minutiae of the Chelmsford train timetable would be well received over someone's Christmas dinner. Post-Christmas it was all finally sorted out. We were then held up by gales in the Bay of Biscay and everyone was going to miss their train, coach, connecting flight to Edinburgh anyway. It was up to the ship's staff to spend the night trying to piece it all together again.

There was also the on-board credit fiasco. We had a list of people with on-board credits, but most of them didn't seem aware of them. The ship had a different list of passengers with on-board credits, and some passengers who didn't appear on either list were adamant that they had been promised them. The sorting out of cabins, credits, and transport, with no help from head office and on top of all the usual problems, was a nightmare. I think as I recall this, of all the passengers who asked how they too could get this – 'it's just a holiday really … admit it' – job.

I did wonder what sort of people went cruising at Christmas. The answer is of course that the vast majority were lovely, cheery people, who thought it would be great, and they were right. It was the only Christmas and New Year when everything fitted in with that picture that you have in your head: carols on Christmas Eve, great decorations, huge Christmas tree, gourmet Christmassy food at every meal, a pantomime on Boxing Day, a great New Year's Eve party on deck with a background of fireworks over Madeira. You didn't get that niggling feeling that you weren't actually … happy enough, or suspect that everyone else was having a better time than you. Best of all, you were not responsible for any of it – whether the turkey was done, whether there were enough mince pies, was auntie overdoing it with the sherry? Nor did you need to worry about what coat or shoes you needed if it was raining en route to the party.

Yes, most people had a great time, but there were a handful, and a bigger handful than usual, who you knew, just knew, were there because nobody would want to spend Christmas with them – this is what I had suspected.

Watching and dealing with thousands of people, you can't help noticing things.

What I noticed was that happy people are people who look for things to be happy about, and that miserable people are people who look for things to be miserable about. I couldn't help noticing who enjoyed themselves and who didn't, and it had precious little to do with the lighting, the food, or whether everything was perfect. In fact it bore no relationship to circumstances at all, and was often in direct contrast.

I remember a lovely couple, relaxed, chatting to me about what a good time they were having – glance at watch.

"Well time for our Guinness now – we always have a Guinness about now – it's our little treat." They wandered off, smiling, arm in arm. I knew, and they knew, that he was suffering from terminal cancer.

Other people can stay furious for days, sometimes the whole holiday, because they didn't get the cabin that they were expecting, or the cabin steward kept forgetting their ice. I was always saying,

"Yes I know your train seats weren't reserved, but you're here now, don't let it spoil your holiday – it's not worth it." Unfortunately they often couldn't see this.

I remember one couple who had been on a side trip that involved a flight, and a night off the ship. The return flight had been delayed and the husband felt that they had not been treated well at the airport, they had not been offered coffee it seemed. He arrived back on board livid. I listened to him fuming for half an hour.

"Look," I said, "it's over now, I'll follow it up and try to sort out what went wrong, but forget it, you don't want it to spoil the rest of your holiday, do you?"

"I don't care," he said, "I'm not forgetting this." And off he went again.

I remembered in happier times, he'd told me very touchingly, how much he loved his wife –

"I worship the ground she walks on," he'd said. How often do men say that – before their wives die? I could have wept.

"Well do you want to spoil your wife's holiday as well?"

"Er ... no ... oh, forget it ... let's have a drink."

But it didn't just teach me about other people; it taught me about myself too. Horror of horrors, I could sometimes see shades of myself in some of these people who I knew were getting it wrong. Wasn't I quick to complain? Didn't I have a tendency to fret for too long over little things? What I learned was – if something is wrong – of course try to get it put right, but if you can't – let it go, forget it – life's too short.

Another thing too, that irritated me, was people checking things for unexpected expense. 'Was breakfast in the cabin, extra?' It wasn't, but I always felt like saying,

"Oh for goodness sake, if you fancied it why didn't you just get it – you're on holiday."

Hang on, wouldn't I have checked? Yes I would. Mental note to take my own advice in future. You can be too careful.

I learned something else too. How to make decisions quickly. Something I was not good at. I'd pace around my cabin, knowing that when I came out I had to have decided what to do about the man sitting in his bed saying that he was ready to die. Could he just hold on until he got home? I didn't like to mention my paperwork. Or the man who was already dead.

Another surprise was that people die on cruises. Not the odd one every now and then, but there was one death on average every cruise. No, nobody is buried at sea now, but if it is any comfort, the person who died always seemed to have had a lovely last day – and always – it was never anybody that had a medical history as long as your arm, and that you had worried about. I don't want to encourage people to put dying on board a cruise ship on their list of things to do, but it's not a bad way to go, and they are all very used to dealing with it, and supportive.

Occasionally a death on board can have unexpected consequences. I remember an elderly lady travelling with her even more elderly mother. She didn't seem to be having much fun. Mother died, and as always, everyone rallies round to help. In this case the captain taking her under his wing, and all the officers, and entertainers asking her to dance, and joining her for dinner, seemed to go some way to compensate for her loss.

I learned so much, and was going to need it all, and more, in my next big job. I had been going to sea, and to see, for twelve years in all, very on and off – two weeks here, three weeks there. I needed to be at home occasionally for more than the obvious reasons. I had taken on a job that was to be the ultimate in stress, panic, and sheer misery. My ability to have what at the time seemed good ideas, but which were in reality, really bad ideas, had peaked – I had thought it would be a good idea to build our own house. But before we descend into that world of muddy wellingtons, and twanging nerves, lets leapfrog over it, fast forward in time, and get on board for one last cruise. It won't take long, as it happens.

Long after I had finished working on cruise ships, my husband and I decided to give cruising a try as passengers. How satisfying it would be to walk away from unpleasant, moaning people. Let people's birthdays, illnesses, deaths, pass me by, as I did exactly as I pleased. I could even behave badly myself if I felt like it … what luxury.

The trip was six weeks, yes, rather a long time for a 'let's give it a try'. But there would be nice food, wine, no hassle for husband, and two weeks exploring the Amazon for me. Seemed a good compromise.

First stop was a freezing, wet morning in Amsterdam. Second stop was a couple of hours wandering round the dock area of Lisbon looking for a postcard for grandchildren. Didn't spend longer, as I thought I'd better see the ship's doctor about flashing lights that had appeared in my eye.

The ship's doctor was charming, and Greek. He reckoned my eye was in better shape than his, but he was rather concerned about my low pulse rate. He would monitor it for a while. Come back next morning. Next morning it was still low, and my blood pressure was looking a little too good to be true in a woman of my age. His advice: eat five times a day, use plenty of salt, drink lots of coffee, stay away from the gym and exercise classes. This was strangely at odds with my pre-cruise get fit regime, and I was really getting into the swing of keeping fit on board. Though using the gym was rather strange, as it was the gym I remembered so well as my surreal viewpoint on the Antarctic.

I returned to the medical centre that evening, having dutifully added mid morning snacks, and tea-time cream cakes to my already ample food intake. The doctor was still not happy. He decided to do an electrocardiogram. This did not reassure him. He sent it off to a 24 hour shore based cardiac back-up unit. They were not happy about it either. He decided to keep me in the medical centre overnight, and keep monitoring. Things did not get better. The offending pulse rate dropped to 42.

"They are very worried about you," he relayed, comfortingly.

There were two very strange aspects to the whole thing. One ... here I was in the very same bed as the passenger who had had the misfortune to spend her Antarctic trip, suffering from pneumonia. And two ... I felt absolutely fine.

The problem was that my pulse rate was either that of a very fit young athlete, or that of someone approaching cardiac arrest, and even I knew that meant death. I could hardly blame them for assuming the latter. It did rather irritate me that all the tests had ... Age 73, at the top, when I was actually only ... nearly ... 73, but that stolen couple of months hardly nudged me into the 'very fit young athlete' category.

As the night wore on, things didn't improve.

"Lie still ... relax ... don't even go to the bathroom." None of these was easy, or even possible given that I was now attached to a drip and an oxygen mask.

By morning it was decided that I needed to be admitted to a cardiac hospital. I might have lasted on board for a bit longer, but Tenerife was the next port of call, and after that it was Cape Verde, four days at sea, and then two weeks in the Amazon. I knew of course that picking a good place to be hospitalised was important.

The puzzling thing was that I still felt fine. I felt fine enough as I was stretchered off the ship and towards the waiting ambulance to say to the ship's photographer at the bottom of the gangway, that I wouldn't be wanting a commemorative photo of my departure. I felt fine enough, when the doctor pressed his card into my hand, to say that I would try not to die still clutching it, as it might reflect badly on him. So grateful was he apparently, that he leapt into the ambulance, kissed my hand, and told me how much he liked me. I thought this was nice of him, as he had been up most of the night worrying about me.

The ambulance screamed off through the streets of Tenerife, siren wailing, to deposit me in an emergency unit. They tested, scanned, X rayed (incidentally the only pictorial record of my trip). As I lay on the trolley covered in electrodes, and still mysteriously feeling fine, I was bewildered as to how I had got here, now being admitted to the cardiac unit.

After 24 hours of monitoring and testing, they could find nothing wrong with me. Only it seemed an excess of fitness. This was to be borne out by further testing when I got back to the UK.

By the time I was discharged from the hospital, the ship was heading towards Cape Verde and the Amazon, and it wasn't possible to rejoin it.

So, it had turned out that I was just too fit for my age. Could I blame anyone for not recognising this ... no.

The ship's doctor had told a story about Niki Lauda the Formula 1 racing driver. It seems that he was found to have a pulse rate of 39, causing alarm and panic, and ambulances to be summoned. Turned out he was just super fit. Niki and I seemed to be pulse buddies. Did this mean I could look forward to a new career as a racing driver? Mmm, unlikely. We were kind of approaching things from opposite directions, because by this time I was not driving at all, so I walked and cycled everywhere.

Wow ... it was keeping me fit. Too fit for a cruise to the Amazon it seemed.

What an ending to my shipboard life.

Chapter Twenty-three

I approach the prospect of writing about self building, with enormous apprehension and a sinking heart. The experience that I had expected to be creative, fulfilling, and ultimately financially uplifting was one of such undiluted trauma, that I have declined invitations to speak on the subject, avoided any writing on the subject, and have tried only partially successfully, to blot it from my memory. So it is with great trepidation that I now start to pick off the scab, and probe the barely healed wounds. I am inviting you to share my pain – you could always refuse my invitation.

It seemed a good idea, and actually unlike many of my ideas, it was a good idea – in theory.

Our current house I had fallen in love with as soon as I had walked through the door. Its odd design was accounted for, I was told, by the fact that it had been built as a prize in a Daily Mail competition – as a prize, note – not prizewinning. It seemed that the builders had been forced by the planners to build it further back from the road than they wanted to, so in a fit of pique they had built it backwards. After all, no-one was going to turn their noses up at a free house, built backwards or forwards. This accounted for the kitchen and bathroom facing the road, and the front door being round the back, facing the back garden. It also meant that all the main rooms faced the garden too – I loved it. A lot of my love though was because of the very large garden. Now that the children had left home, the house was too big for us, and my husband was getting fed up with the constant maintenance, and the fact that it took best part of a day to cut all the grass. We liked our town, we liked the fact that we were only five minutes cycle ride from the centre, and most of our friends now, lived here – we would really like to stay right here. We didn't feel ready for the two bed bungalows in the vicinity, they seemed to have 'old people' writ large over them. This is when I started looking at the idea of self build.

We had an impressive list of things already, that self builders would give their right arm for – well perhaps not 'right arm' it is kind of useful to a self builder.

For some long forgotten reason, we had a gap down one side of our house which would give access across our own land to the 'new plot'. We had a plot exactly where we wanted it; we already owned it, so it would cost us nothing. An estate agent had assured us that if we got it right, we would not lower the value of our current house as big gardens were as much a liability as a plus point. We would end up with two houses each in a quarter acre plot, surely that would be acceptable to the planners. We could live in comfort in our present house while overseeing the new build – no caravan or discomfort needed. The plot was secluded and pretty, surrounded by trees, hedges, and other people's gardens. This last of course – surrounded by other people's gardens – was a prickly point. Nobody, and I understand it, likes to have their view of other people's gardens interfered with – the dreaded, 'back-land development'. I rang the planning office.

"Whenever you see the words – 'back-land development' they are always preceded by the word – 'undesirable'. Does this mean:

That this is a particular piece of back-land development that is undesirable, or

That back-land development is by its very nature always undesirable?"

I waited with bated breath – the project hung on this. It was the former. Systems go.

We were determined to do it right. First we would visit all the neighbours involved, tell them what we had in mind – a low rise dormer bungalow with no windows overlooking them, designed to cause minimal impact on them and their outlook, and that we would address any concerns they had.

Our first neighbour wished us well – it wasn't going to bother her. Neighbours on the other side pointed out themselves, that they were barely going to see it because of the trees and hedges – perhaps just the chimney? The wife pointed out that it was just the sort of thing that they would have wanted to do themselves. So far so good – well actually no – they turned out to be amongst our most active opponents. There were three other bungalows involved to the side, all with long gardens running down to our plot. One considered selling us the bottom bit of her long narrow garden. She never ventured down there; it was a tangle of old fruit trees and brambles. She would barely be able to see our proposed build either, she admitted. She also turned out to be a vehement protester. The other two were not very happy from the word go. I know the bottom of our garden was a bit wild, but to see it described as a 'wilderness area' and therefore of huge value to the planet, was a bit hurtful. Also this man pointed out that although he wouldn't see much in the way of a building, he was retiring soon and wasn't planning on us being in this part of our garden much anyway, as it would interfere with his enjoyment of his own garden. His neighbour was later to object to our use of a roof light window facing in his direction. He pointed out that although he knew that the offending window was six feet from the floor and that we wouldn't be able to see through it – they would still have the feeling that they were being overlooked. What on earth did they get up to? Perhaps it would be worth dragging a chair to the roof light and having a look.

Things seemed, at that point, to have gone quite well. After all, developers had been sniffing round this area of back gardens for years and their plans had been for whole estates of houses. Perhaps people realised that we were saving them from the developers and blocking access to further development. No they didn't.

As I only had one job now, the intermittent cruising, I reckoned I had room for another – we would manage this project ourselves.

I'd be good at organising and supervising it all, I thought happily. As usual I had forgotten one large, personal stumbling block. I am indecisive to what is possibly a clinical degree. Choosing between shades of beige for a carpet could take months, years even, as could decisions about teaspoons, curtains, and coffee tables. Undeterred, well actually unaware, of the ramifications of this character flaw, I set about designing my own house and everything in it. Everything – being down to the last tap fitting, position of the last light switch, tiles, wall ties, floor construction – everything, and decisions needed ... fast.

First we needed to get outline planning permission. To do this you needed to show some sort of a footprint. You can't have a footprint without a foot. I began tinkering about with designs. We had decided roughly what we wanted – something traditional, cottagey – a bit roses round the door, I'm embarrassed to admit. Well we are old people, we are allowed roses round the door. I wanted something too that was really integrated into the garden, a door to a little walled garden perhaps, lots of light coming from all directions, a minstrel's gallery, an inglenook ... oo ... it was really exciting. You get to know what you don't want as well. I didn't want a long through living room; I wanted something cosier with lots of comfortable seating, and no doors in it to anywhere else. I didn't want a huge kitchen either, I'd had two and although they looked impressive they didn't work. I always ended up working in an L shaped bit in one corner between doors. No kitchen through-doors either then, a U-shaped kitchen where you could reach both sides.

It might sound as if I had plenty to go on and would find designing such a dwelling a doddle – no.

There were too many options and none worked out perfectly – morning sun in the kitchen, garage to the north etc. Still outline permission was not totally binding, let's just put in for it with something, and sweat out the details later. Our proposal was quite modest. The planning office could see no problem with it, and passed it. We were euphoric. Too soon.

By now the opposition from neighbours had been swelled by people who lived over the road, and objected to additional traffic. I knew we couldn't guarantee that we would never sell it, and people might move in whose main form of transport was not two bikes, but it was a three bedroom retirement type bungalow, hardly likely to give rise to streams of articulated lorries. Then there were the people who wouldn't be affected in any way, but who objected on principle. A council site meeting was called. Muttering neighbours and other 'interested parties' gathered outside our house. Only one councillor seemed to see anything to object to.

"Come on Jack," I heard one of the others say, "you could get a block of flats in here."

The planning council rejected our application.

What now? We couldn't back track to anything more modest. Perhaps we should have applied for three houses and then could have pulled back to one, and everyone would have been happy. We either dropped it or went to appeal. We decided to appeal. In due course the Government Appeal Inspector came, inspected, and said he couldn't see anything to object to, and passed it.

Perhaps a note on time here – everything takes a long time. The planning office needs time; the council has long lists of applications to consider, and only meets twice a month. The appeal took the best part of a year. We are now more than eighteen months from first move to this point. This is not, we were learning, something that you could do in a hurry.

We really seriously now, needed to decide on the plans, and the method of building and how we were going to organise things. There was a bewildering choice. We read self-building magazines, went to self-build exhibitions. Did we want timber frame, poured concrete walls, oak frame, hay bale walls, grass roof, concrete raft, concrete beamed floor? Did we want someone to do the whole lot – what if we fell out with the builder early on? Did we want to do a lot of it ourselves? Too difficult. Did we need an architect? Site manager?

We wasted a lot of people's time at this stage I'm afraid. In the unlikely event of any of them reading this I apologise. The trouble was that when you made an enquiry, in order to give you any idea of what they could do for you, or what it would cost, they had to do quite a lot of work, and then ... mmm ... not too sure. That oak frame house was cute, but was it a bit twee for this suburban site, and did we want all our garden in front of it like that? Timber frame? Would local workers understand how careful you had to be not to puncture that waterproof membrane? Then local timber-frame houses made the national news, with a fire that whipped down the whole row. Mmm ... no timber-frame then. We were beginning to lean towards a traditional brick build. Although my ten or so design ideas were whittling down, making that final decision was so difficult. Perhaps a real architect was what we needed. An architect might come up with some unexpected brilliant solutions and the design issue would be resolved.

We tracked down an architect who was recommended as having a particular interest in self builders. I was itching to see what – 'well I never thought of that,' ideas he would come up with. Apart from the intriguing, trendy, but eventually we decided, impractical ideas of some floor level horizontal strip windows, and a bedroom balcony which overhung the kitchen for its entire length, nothing much. We do have a bit of balcony overhanging our breakfast room, and very difficult it is too to keep smells of burning toast out of this room, or to remember at breakfast not to talk about visitors lying in bed above you, or not to disturb sleeping grandchildren, with your evening revelries.

After viewing these ideas, I decided that my final – it had to be final, I was running out of life – design was as good as anything he had thought of. He should just draw it up and let's move on.

Easier said than done. Everything took weeks if not months. He always seemed to be in Wales, or abroad. He was very busy, obviously. The work, we suspected was being done by his two apprentices – supervised? We didn't know. They appeared to sleep on the premises in a crumpled, untidy looking room that we caught sight of once. They both had a strange blank eyed look, and a kind of strange slow demeanour. Was this why the plans arrived with the two full length vertical windows on either side of the fireplace, recumbent in horizontal mode? It had taken months to receive these plans, and when we sent them back for correction this was to be just the first of many such, unhappy returns. They would arrive back, after numerous phone calls, weeks or months later with the windows corrected, but a door in the wrong place, or the scale wrong, or something else wrong. Months dragged by. As each amended mistake was accompanied by each new mistake, we began to feel that we were going crazy. Was it us, or was it him? It was him – he would have to go. As was to happen more than once in the future, he seemed hurt, and mystified as to our dissatisfaction.

We started looking for someone else. I was by now satisfied with my plans, we just needed someone to draw them up. Local builders, we discovered used this man, well no he wasn't an architect, but he was good at drawing up plans. Lots of people had had their extension or garage plans drawn up by him. That was what we wanted, someone hands on, practical, and preferably close at hand. Again something had slipped through our logic net. What he was good at was drawing plans for garages and extensions. This was a small but seriously complicated house. The architect had told me that I could have anything design-wise that I wanted – everything was possible. While strictly speaking that might be true, upstairs rooms that don't correspond to downstairs rooms, unsupported features at all angles and in all places, present a problem to the builder and to the draughtsman. For example the large, open, double height hall, in the centre of the house, needed huge steel beams and an equally huge crane to position them. And no, we couldn't have this space supported by oak beams – thank goodness his structural engineer stood up to us on that one. Our man agreed that he could do this and we gave him the go ahead. He wouldn't do detailed instructions for those odd bits that might need detailed instructions, how exactly the brickwork should be done at junctions with steel beams etc. Why would we need them we thought? The brickies stuck all day usually, doing boring, repetitive things would relish surely the opportunity to exercise their problem solving capacities – a happy opportunity to create something different of which they would be proud. Not so – oh how not so! Bricklayers want to stand putting one brick on top of the other, their minds happily elsewhere, on the football, the girlfriend, or their hangover. Also, thinking about things takes time – time is money – there are four other jobs waiting. This was yet another thing we got wrong. Is there no end to them? Unfortunately – no.

We thought that we would be bestowing our work onto a hungry and grateful workforce, eager to work on our interesting project – not so either. We quickly learned that builders were doing us a favour even considering working for us. This was partly because of the inherent stumbling blocks already outlined, and partly because a previous building slump had caused a significant number of workers in the building industry to move to other jobs and there was a severe shortage of them.

We had read a lot about how to ensure that you drew up contracts that would protect you if things went wrong, or work dragged on.

'Always get everything in writing,' was the advice. 'Finishing dates, penalty clauses for failure to finish on time, detailed costings – lay out clearly what your expectations are and get the builder to sign this document.'

On the ground, in the real world, things were very different.

"I was talking to one man," confided the builder that we were interviewing ..." 'e wanted to tie me down to a finishing date," he snorted, "and penalty clauses – wanted to fine me for getting behind with the work ... what a bleedin' cheek! I told him what he could do with his bleedin' job!"

We clucked sympathetically, and dishonestly.

"Came back to me later he did, all apologetic like. Told me he'd drop all the finishing times and penalty stuff – would I do it for him ... please? Would I? I would not. I wasn't going to work for a geezer like that."

We surreptitiously slid our pages of conditions, under the self-build magazines and sympathised.

Months were wasted trying to get a builder interested. We thought that we would get the shell up by using one builder and then tackle the fitting out with subcontractors. We reasoned that we didn't want to give the entire thing to one builder. What would happen if he turned out to be unsatisfactory and we were stuck with him. Being 'stuck' with someone turned out to be the antithesis of the problem. We sent our plans to a lot of builders. The builders that we really wanted said that they were busy for the next six months but could do it then. Six months! Heavens we'd be hanging curtains by then. One wanted to order the materials himself – we could do that we thought – shop around, save money. He wasn't interested then. We went off another when he suggested a dozen soak-aways, and when after some research we reduced it to four, said it would cost the same. We didn't like the sound of that. One was suspiciously cheap, one was jaw-droppingly expensive.

We did realise afterwards that we were asking the impossible. Give us a quote we said, bearing in mind that we would like to work alongside you and help. Well this was a poisoned chalice if ever there was one. How did they know what we could do, or how much? Assume we would be a real help and quote low, and find we weren't, and were always in bed, or going off to France, or assume we were going to be no help and quote high, and not get the job. Besides the last thing any workman would want is a pair of amateurs working alongside them, even if it was just fetching and carrying or clearing up. No, that was a crazy idea.

We settled finally on a nice man who seemed despite his nervous manner, keen and interested. He had worked for other satisfied people we knew (again small jobs) and showed us a barn conversion he had done. The work looked excellent. The all exposed beams on the walls and roof looked great, but not for our little suburban house. This is where a misunderstanding seemed to arise. We had told him we wanted a few oak beams.

"Just enough to hang bunches of herbs on," he had said, exposing our naffness – yes he had got our measure. So why was he going out to get the huge number of wall and ceiling beams that he thought we needed? We queried this. He did not look happy. It was only a small misunderstanding surely.

On day two of the groundwork, with diggers, dumpers, and lorries on site and working industriously – at last we were getting started – he said that he needed to speak to us. He had a problem. Fine, there were bound to be little problems to sort out.

"I'm losing sleep over this job," he said. "Sorry I can't go on " and he walked out. We were stunned. He had told us that he had packed up building for a time as he had found it too stressful. Why hadn't we listened? Meanwhile the workers and machinery were still blithely unaware. We had to go down and break the news to the digger, dumper, and lorry, drivers. They were stunned too. Work stopped, they wandered off taking their machinery with them.

Not surprisingly the other builders that we now went back to, were not interested.

I looked in the yellow pages, and contacted a nearby construction firm. Enough of small players. We needed the safety of a big firm, that wouldn't panic, and wouldn't go home and take its ball with it, at the first problem. This firm was called something farm, perhaps we could tip some of the huge amount of soil being displaced by our need for six foot foundations, around the farm. Turned out it wasn't really a farm but we liked the man we met, and yes he would be personally responsible for the project, and they had at their disposal several groups of tried and tested builders. It would be no problem. A price was agreed – we would buy the materials – he would oversee the building of the shell. Then just before work started, he phoned us. He had parted company with the firm, he said. Good manners seemed to have prevented us from enquiring why. He was starting out on his own. We could either stay with the firm or come with him. We had never met anyone else in the firm, and we liked him, and, fatally, trusted him – we'd go with him.

A group of ground-workers turned up, and no messing, got on with the ground works. A large crane had to be brought in, to position the concrete floor beams that I had ordered thinking that we could lift and lay them ourselves. I had managed to find a farmer who would take all our expensive to tip soil. We really liked the leader of the gang too – Gary. He was positive and bright, and was organising things well. Then one week he wasn't there.

"Where's Gary?"

"Oh, he's gone to another job in London – it's going to take months." Could a contract have stopped that happening, even if we had thought of it, and someone had been prepared to sign it?

Without Gary the work suffered. A bit of the foundation was not in quite the right place. The insurance inspector explained in graphic detail how a wall that was not quite central on its foundation, could rotate the foundation onto its side, bringing down the wall, and eventually the house presumably with it. But it would probably be alright, not really worth re-doing it.

Nightmares about rotating foundations were not our only problem at this time. We had gone to a lot of trouble choosing the bricks – well, choosing everything actually – driving all over the country to see things in situ. The brick manufacturers had been so helpful, that although we could have ordered the bricks from our local builders' merchant for the same price, along with the other stuff, I decided to give them the order direct. I wasn't too happy about sending off the cheque for the full amount in advance, but their system they explained was – they receive the cheque one day and the bricks are dispatched the next. The firm had been trading for ninety nine years for goodness sake. I must learn to stop worrying. But we got a worrying phone call on the morning the bricks were to arrive … er … they were having a bit of a problem … the bricks wouldn't be coming today … What was the problem?… Where was our money?… don't worry … it would be OK. Unfortunately it wasn't OK. This ninety nine year old firm had gone bust on the day our cheque arrived. If our cheque had arrived the day before, the bricks would have been dispatched. If it had arrived the next day or even by second post on that fateful day, the firm's bank account would already have been frozen. There was just that one morning in ninety nine years when our money could be lost – and it was.

I seem to remember sobbing down the phone that I was a pensioner – what I thought that had to do with it I can't now remember – we had lost £3,000. Over the next five or six years we got a couple of cheques for a few pounds back, we were the only private individuals involved in this bankruptcy it seemed. That was surely the baddest of bad luck, but nevertheless we had to find the money for the bricks again.

Acquisition of the bricks was not the only problem we had with bricks. We were to discover that dealing with most workmen was a matter of infinite delicacy, but that brickies were the undisputed prima donnas of the building world. My apologies to brickies' wives, mothers, and girlfriends in advance. I'm sure they are wonderful husbands, sons, fathers, lovers – peg out the washing, bring you a cup of tea in bed, but on a building site my experience of brickies, and sadly there were to be many of them – both brickies and experiences – were not good. This was an example of how it usually went.

Mortar should not be dropped on the metal wall ties that tie the outer and inner walls together: damp can travel from the outside to the inside. I had read it. Large blobs of mortar were being dropped on the wall ties. Could our 'site manager' tell them not to do it?

"Oh ..." he looked dubious, "they wouldn't like being told that. Workmen don't like being criticised," he added as if by way of explanation. My husband, although he could sometimes be shamed into doing it, hated this task too – telling workmen that you were not happy about something. Not for the last time the job fell to me. There is no right way I discovered to tell a workman particularly a bricklayer anything. Did they say?

"You know what missus, you are absolutely right – silly us, we

just kind of forgot – thanks for taking the trouble to remind us"…
and tip their caps? No, a frostiness settled between us. Being
criticised is bad enough, but by a woman – unforgivable!

I chickened out of asking them not to mix large batches of
mortar just before they packed up for the day, and tipping them
onto what was to be my garden, or to stop using our neighbours
garden as a toilet, when they had been told that they were welcome
to use our comfy, in house, toilet. The latter was probably no
longer a problem as they were probably now peeing into the mortar
… or worse. However timorously you asked brickies anything, it
caused them to go into a major sulk or paddy that lasted
throughout your miserable relationship with them. We ended up
having I think, seven lots of brickies, and they were all as 'teenage
girlie' as each other.

The obvious remedy to this problem would seem to be to just
leave workmen alone to get on with it and hope for the best. We
tried that too. They then saw you as 'soft'. One brickie we were
later to employ on a 'day rate' started coming in so late, spending
so long at the greasy spoon, beloved sanctuary it seemed of all
bricklayers, and going so early that we were lucky to get two or
three hours actual bricklaying out of him. He was nevertheless
furious and indignant, when we sacked him. Another pair we
offered weekend work to, said they would only consider one
weekend day, despite our having to hire the cement mixer on a two
day basis, and when after the previous experience, I asked very
delicately what sort of hours they were considering, flounced off
making no effort to hide their outrage, and were never seen again.

Sometimes they amused themselves, playing games with my
nerves.

"Missus – a problem – see this front wall? Well the two sides
under the gable – they don't match … it's the windows see … it's
going to be all lop sided where you want those fancy bits." We
studied and discussed the 'problem' for about an hour.

"Oh … well … just do the best you can." Why did it have to be
right at the front where you would see it? It turned out to be no

problem at all – looked fine – so why did they do it? Perhaps they just wanted a bit of a rest, and some entertainment.

There were some real problems though. The plans which had had no obvious mistakes, had several non obvious to the naked eye mistakes. The supporting beams for the garage ceiling were shown too high. They'd put them in now – surely I wouldn't want them taken out – it might take days – even weeks were implied. It would only mean that the bedroom above the garage would have a three inch step up to it. No I didn't want a three inch step – yes – I did want them moved; it took half a day.

More shocking – the balcony above the breakfast room was just about to be started when our draughtsman arrived, flustered. Sorry, he'd made a mistake – he'd forgotten about the support pillars being in the way – just brick it all up.

What! This was a major design feature; the room above got half its light through those balcony rails. The whole design of that end of the house depended on it.

"What do you want us to do?" The brickies waited for a decision, bricks in hand, mortar setting.

"Leave as much balcony as you can … " what else could I say? We ended up with a sort of rabbit hole rather than the majestic sweep that I had envisaged. The design had been too much for this designer of extensions – but too late to find out now.

My ultra complicated design caused other problems too. That steel beam we'd needed to support the balcony was now sticking unattractively out of the outside brickwork – was it possible to cut some bricks in half lengthways to cover it? Constructing this little diagonal bit that had looked so cute (and simple) on paper. "How do you want us to do it missus?" How did I?

There was a real problem with the drive too. It was long and narrow and awkward, but worst of all it was on heavy clay. It got very wet and sticky. I knew, I'd tried to grow vegetables in it. Half a mile away they used it straight out of the ground to make bricks. But no-one had ever tried driving cement lorries, or cranes on it, or delivery lorries full of bricks. It had become a quagmire. More than once other lorries had to be dispatched to drag vehicles out of the mire.

But help was at hand – our man had heard something. Our town's new Sainsburys was being built on an existing car park. We could have the excavated car park surface for nothing, just the cost of collecting and transporting it – that was a piece of luck. It would be just the job for stabilizing our semi liquid drive. The car park was dug, transported and ... was immediately sucked into our drive leaving no trace. If anything it was worse than before. Lorries from our builders' merchants were reluctant to put themselves at risk, and didn't want to deliver things. They wanted to leave them on the pavement. The builders didn't want to have to carry stuff down. The car park material had to be dug out, transported to a tip, hefty tipping charges paid, in order to put down a very expensive strengthening fabric, and more hardcore. I say more, because many, many, loads of hardcore had already sunk into the jaws of this rapacious bog.

I have mentioned the inordinate number of bricklayers that we ended up employing. Why did we need them? We already had bricklayers – didn't we ?

I was becoming increasingly concerned about the budget. It seemed to be disappearing at an alarming rate, almost as fast as materials into our drive. A lot of it seemed to be going to chiefs rather than indians.

"Are you sure we are leaving enough money for the roof?" I enquired of our site manager on several occasions.

"Don't you worry about it," – the 'my dear' was not said, but always implied. "I'm the expert remember – I've got it covered."

As it turned out, he didn't have it covered, and there was nowhere near enough left in the kitty to see our house covered by a roof either. The brickwork wasn't even finished, when our site manager announced that the money had run out.

"Sorry," he said, "I've never done this before – it's a steep learning curve for me," – and he walked off and left us. I don't know what happened to him, but I hope that it was nothing good.

Again there was a stand-off. To add insult to injury the builders turned up to take away their scaffolding. Something inside me snapped. A red mist descended.

"The least you can do is leave us the bloody scaffolding," I screamed at them through the gate.

"Sorry missus, the boss says ..."

"Get the boss here – now!"

"He's busy ... he's told us ... we have to ..."

"Don't you dare set foot on this land," I growled as they advanced.

"We'll fetch the police ... "

"Fetch them."

What I thought I would say if they had fetched the police, I don't know. The scaffolding was after all, their property. My husband not one for confrontations, stood behind me. I'm not sure if he was more afraid of the builders, the police, or me.

They capitulated – we could keep the scaffolding till we finished. This turned out to be even more generous of them than they thought, given the length of time before they were to get it back. I would worry about what they would do in the way of damage to our house as they dismantled it ... later.

We now needed to get reorganised. We'd hire our brickies directly, then hopefully just pay for bricklayers, and not non working overseers and absent gang bosses. Hence our aforementioned bricklayer experiences. We also needed to get a new roofer lined up.

I remember the first two roofers who came to give us a quote. I remember them coming back up the drive after examining our walls. They sucked their teeth and shook their heads in that way that was becoming so familiar.

"Sorry love – we can't put a roof on that – no-one could – it's not possible – it's the shape see – you won't do it."

We were stunned. It was not possible to construct a roof for our house!

The trouble with the haphazard way that our build had evolved was that no-one was responsible for anything. Who could we blame for this? No-one. More importantly – what were we to do with a half built, un-finishable house?

By now it was about three years since my first innocent, girlish fancies, as I had skipped down the garden saying … "See … drive here … house here … simple." We had foundations, we had walls, but now we had an impossible to roof, shell. We were exhausted and demoralised.

A winter passed. The gaunt walls rising up, rain lashed, snow covered, reproached us on a daily basis. I lay awake on stormy nights. Would those unsupported gable ends still be standing when I drew the curtains?

I began to notice adverts in building magazines; 'Half finished house for sale' – sometimes relationship break-up was cited. I could understand that. What I really needed at this time was to have a nervous breakdown, and possibly a divorce, but I couldn't afford the luxury of either of these, until the job was done. Even the option of selling was out of reach. Who would buy a set of walls that couldn't be roofed?

Eventually we managed to drag ourselves out of the slough of despond and had another go.

Yes it could be roofed, but not with the more usual factory made trusses – the roof would have to be cut from timber on site. Complicated and more expensive, but at least it could be done. We managed to find a roofer from the dying breed of roofers who could do this. We were almost glad to hear the sickening crashes as bundles of our expensive clay tiles slid off the roof and shattered on the piles of broken bricks below – at least work was progressing. The roof took shape, we had a house … well … a shell.

As is customary I think, the accommodation looked alternately very small and very large as building progressed, but it definitely turned out to be higher than I had expected. A dormer bungalow, I admit can be almost anything. I had drawn the elevations with the roof slope starting at floor level in the upstairs rooms, it meant a lot of the space was too low to use, but we didn't need big bedrooms, and this would keep the roof-line low. Our original architect had said,

"Better add a foot of wall upstairs just in case." Our draughtsman had said,

"Better add another foot of wall upstairs just in case."

The result was nice big upstairs rooms, but given the impossibility to an amateur of imagining height, we ended up with less of a tall bungalow, and more of a short house. Sorry neighbours, we didn't mean to – honest.

Having got the outside done, we looked forward to plainer sailing inside – and heavens above – we were right !

Perhaps after this level of disaster, anything short of our project being hit by a meteorite, or 'builders' crack, bottom rot' wiping out all workmen, anything, would have seemed like good progress. Generally we got on much better with the inside workers. Could they be better tempered due to not being subjected to the elements? Perhaps.

Things started to move – for us – fast. This necessitated the rapid ordering and selecting of a million things. Door fittings that would have taken me weeks to choose – individually – had to be chosen in one fell swoop, in an afternoon. Bathroom fittings for next week ... er ... OK. Tiles, windows, insulation, position of lights. Even the tiniest decision had the potential to cause future repercussions. Visitors are constantly switching off our outside security lights, thinking that they are switching on the light in the downstairs toilet; that looked a logical position for the light switch – clearly it wasn't.

Every evening after the cycle ride to the pub, which was keeping us sane, a list was drawn up of the dozen or so phone calls, orders, and decisions that had to be made the following day. It's exactly what I hate to do, and I had no-one but myself to blame.

I wasn't however to blame for the choice of complicated, 'techie' things that nobody except a few specialist firms knew anything about – underfloor heating, complicated hot water cylinders, central vacuuming systems.

More recently, a plumber who we had asked to look at our heating/hot water system, opened the door to our cylinder cupboard, and turned several shades paler.

"No way I'm touching that," he said, and beat a hasty retreat.

Endless, indigestion inducing, sketches were scribbled on the backs of envelopes while we ate. We calculated the underfloor allowance for the heating ourselves – would it work? There was only a half inch tolerance for the dog-leg staircase – had I got it right?

We were doing a lot of the 'dogs-body' work ourselves – it was exhausting and we often got things wrong. Was it worth it? I doubt it. It would take us a week to do something that could be done in half a day by someone who knew what they were doing.

We were beginning to understand too, why we spent so many mornings sleepily waiting at the gates at 7.30am for workmen who didn't turn up for days, or sometimes weeks, with no warning and no explanation. Why did they hate our house? Why did they hate us? Our plasterer at least had the decency to explain.

"Sorry, I won't be able to start on Monday after all ... yes I know I promised ... yes I know you have already waited for weeks ... truth is Bloggs the builders have asked me to do some work for them – quick. They are in a position to offer me more work in the future ... you aren't ... it's unfair I know but, sorry ... see you in about a month." This piece of honesty from a guy we really liked, explained a lot.

We liked our electrician too. He gave us lots of helpful advice, and sent in loads of people so that amazingly the job was done really quickly – how often could I say that?

Our plumber was great too. Mind you I would say that even if he wasn't. Nobody else could understand our system, and when he retires we have had it. Even so, he and I had our moments. Carrying a tray of tea down to the new house one day, I saw clouds of white steam issuing in a great plume from the kitchen wall into my already much loved circular walled garden.

"Chosen a new Pope have you?" I said cheerily as I plonked the tray down, "Gosh good job this is only a run through ... hard to imagine how even a new boiler could make so much steam..."

There was a furtive down-casting of eyes. I froze in horror.

"This is just a start up ... run through?"

"It's a condensing boiler ... it will do this all the time."

Not in my circular walled garden it won't. I was adamant. I was going to sit and eat my breakfast in my south east facing haven, surrounded by my choicest and most scented flowers, with a wall fountain tinkling into a hand thrown pot. How was this now visible dream going to take place? Five foot plumes of boiler steam did not feature in this idyll. It would have to go. Who was responsible for our lack of knowledge re clouds of steam was hotly debated for months, but, I was having it moved – no question. Given the aforementioned complexity of the system, levels were important; it would be difficult to make the boiler a bedroom feature. The only place for it was on the far wall of the garage at the other end of the house. All the piping would have to be reversed it might take weeks, and could not be tackled for months. The wait was long, but as usual the job took a day. As it happened, due to bad boiler design, the boiler had burnt itself out in a few years and we reverted to an ordinary one. Would the plumber like to put it back in the kitchen? I enquired mischievously. His answer was unprintable.

Problems, though fewer, were clearly still arising, but people didn't usually frighten me. There was one occasion when they did.

We had employed a chippie to hang the internal doors. Yet again he came recommended, this time by a friend. "He's lovely," she said, "and he's got all these big brothers who look out for him; he's the baby of the family." He was a big baby – about six foot four, and he duly came to size up the job. We warned him several times that the doors were oak. We knew oak was hard to work with and that extra time would probably need to be factored in. It would take three days he said, and gave us a quote. Fine. See you Monday. On Monday he turned up with a mate who was going to help him. We were immediately aware that the teeth sucking had started. His friend said that the quote was not enough.

"...They're oak, you see missus ... takes longer to work with, does oak."

"Yes I know ... but I told him ..."

It was to no avail. The teeth sucking and head shaking, and muttering, went on all day. That evening we decided to pay them for the day's work, and get someone else. My husband broke the news by phone. I could tell by the way he held the earpiece away from his ear that our man was not happy. It seemed that everyone knew that when you priced a job for three days, you were going to do most of it on the first day, so that wasn't fair, and anyway he didn't believe that we were going to send him a cheque. He was coming round with his brothers – now. I'm not sure whether he mentioned that the intention was to duff us up, but it was certainly implied. I was scared. It was my husband this time who was brave. He assured me that it would be alright. He stood outside with the money while I hid in the toilet with the door locked. The guy must have calmed down by the time he arrived. Husband was still standing, and un-duffed when I ventured out.

Eventually this nightmare, this albatross that had hung around our necks for at least five years was over. Amazingly, given its chequered past we have had few problems with the house. Given the rate of build, we even had the bonus of no drying out cracks; after all it had plenty of time to dry out – really, really, slowly. It all turned out all right ... eventually. Nobody asked though if we would like to do it again. Would that be as opposed to being boiled alive in a vat of camel's entrails then? But people have pointed out that as we now have a nice house, exactly what, and where we want, surely in the end it was worth it. Much as I love the house, delightful as it is to live in, and even though I have forgiven it the pain it caused, nothing ... but ... nothing, is worth waking up every morning for five years with either a sinking heart, or feeling sick with worry. Full stop.

Given that a lot of the problems were caused by our own mistakes, and that we surely had more than our share of bad luck – would I recommend self build to anyone else? No.

Chapter Twenty-four

Now I have to address some questions that have increasingly niggled at the back of my mind as I have been writing.

Who have I written all this for? And perhaps more importantly – what have I written it for?

There is another problem that has arisen too. It has become increasingly obvious that gathering together all these experiences, has uncovered the fact that I seem to have been even more prone to foolish mistakes than even I had been aware of. Do I want this brought to the attention of a wider audience than just myself? Perhaps I had better tackle this last point first, because if I can't resolve it, there is no point considering the others.

What tends to happen in life is that your mistakes are apportioned out. Everyone you know might know of a couple, but happily no-one knows them all. I have kind of short circuited this self preservation mechanism.

I have belonged for many years to a women's organisation – 'Women's Register'. It is mainly a sort of discussion group, and meets in members' houses. One evening the subject was diaries. We were all to bring and read from one, our own, or someone else's. By-passing Pepys, Adrian Mole, and even 'A Nobody,' I read from one of my own. I think it must have been the account of the scooter trip. When I had finished, there was an awkward silence. Then someone said,

"You were very … naïve … weren't you?" The groping for the word was clearly brought about by the need to avoid the obvious choice of the word … 'stupid'. Do I want my grandchildren to know how, 'naïve' their grandmother was?

But then, why not know that your grandmother was a human being – prone – even very prone, to making mistakes? Perhaps it will help them when making mistakes of their own to know that it probably isn't their fault at all, but due to a faulty inherited gene over which they have no control. My friends obviously know me well enough already, and my family, to not be very surprised. What about strangers? Will people that I don't know end up reading this anyway? If so should I worry about what they might think of me? Perhaps that is a bit of vanity ... and unlikely. Though, perhaps ... now here's a thought ... perhaps reading about my shortcomings might even *help* people. Make them feel better about themselves. Cause them to put down the gun, or take their head out of the oven. Perhaps result in such headlines as:

'How I saved lives, explains influential, life guru author, Ruth Jennings!'

'Psychiatric wards close, as general feeling of self worth sweeps the country.'

'This book has changed my life – I thought I was hopeless, till I realised that there is someone out there much worse than me.'

I will therefore sacrifice myself to the general good! Literally, perhaps – publish and be damned.

Unburdening myself of this 'catalogue of mistakes' revelation, to a friend, she said,

"Haven't you said anything good about yourself ... good mother ... good ... anything?"

"Actually ... no."

"Well that's ridiculous."

Perhaps it is – so here goes.

We have a family black joke born of news reports of mothers defending errant sons:

"He's a good boy really ... he's never killed a policeman before."

So ... I have never killed a policeman. I have managed to stay married to the same man for fifty years, and despite everything he still wants to stay married to me. My two sons, independently, unprompted, and without threats of violence, have stated that they couldn't have had a better childhood. (They haven't killed a policeman either.) I am not involved in any family feuds. I have lots of good friends, many of whom have been friends for more than thirty years.

I have had another revelation ... these are the important things surely?

Whew! Take own head out of oven – switch off gas – hand in gun at next gun amnesty.

So that brings me to – who have I actually written this for?

Firstly I suppose, I have written it for myself. My angry interventions at literature class, about who exactly, some tortuously convoluted and opaque book has been written for, seem to have established that an author is entitled to write for themselves, with consideration of the reader coming a poor second, or not entering the frame at all.

I felt a sudden urge to write down everything that I thought might be interesting, before I forgot it. Will some kind person at some future date, read it back to me? Will I say,

"Oh she seems to have had an interesting life ... who was she again?"

Have I been writing for my grandchildren? But my grandchildren have been born in America, and no doubt will grow up as Americans. What possible connection would they feel to events and attitudes that I have sometimes had difficulty connecting with, myself?

However, I remember that it was in the 1980s that I first began getting interested in what my own grandmother's life must have been like a hundred years before, in the 1880s, and that was in another country and another culture. Perhaps, who knows, in 2050 my grandchildren might be just of that age to be interested in my life in 1950s England.

Have I been writing for my own children, and family? Partly, of course. But why then my strange reluctance to use names – is it a caution born of *In the Bin*?

Right, question three – what have I written it for?

Two things have increasingly impinged upon my consciousness – first the enormous changes in life since the '40s, and second that everyone should be writing down their own memories. They should be writing them down and giving them to someone that they can trust to keep them safe. A friend's aunt had a collection of letters from her friend who had been a missionary in China at the beginning of the last century. Eighty years later, tidying up … she burned them.

In this age of emails and text messages what are future generations going to know about life now? Will photos held on computers survive? We don't do those wonderful – whole family put on their best clothes and visit the photographer – photos. And if my own photo collection is anything to go by, what's left will be pictures of nameless beaches, buildings, and hillsides, and smiling groups of nameless people. Oh, and lots of photos of celebratory meals. Will future generations deduce that in our house we hardly ever had a decent meal, so when we did, we felt we needed to record the event for posterity. Oh dear!

But what life was like – could they imagine? Life in the last century is beginning to seem strange already to me. How are they going to imagine it? Rationing for instance.

"Huh! … sweets off the ration – that will never work – they'll never be able to keep up with demand," I remember saying. My sister locking away her butter ration in the bookcase because she thought she wasn't getting her fair share. Then unlocking it when she realised that she was getting more. Five of us solemnly sharing the first banana I ever saw. The fact that as a teenager I used to walk ten minutes to the nearest phone box to make, and receive, pre-arranged calls. No texting, emailing, Facebook. No house phone.

All these little things will be lost. Does it matter? I think it does. The only written memories left will be the flood of books about abusive childhoods, and celebrities.

We Lived in Prime Minister's Dustbin … Elvis's Secret Marriage to a Martian … Pope Forced Me to Have His Love-child. Do we want to be remembered by only these? Don't we need some other memories to balance it out a bit?

Equally, at the other end of the sensation scale are all those blogs and video diaries. To echo my old friend from The Liverpool Echo 'One thing I do know – they will never last.' Seriously though, if they do, how interesting will it be in fifty years time to know that someone got up had breakfast, and went to the pub after work. And what about all the pictures of people's cats and dogs, and their names? Hang on, perhaps I am missing something here. Perhaps this is also valuable social history. Didn't I call my childhood cat 'Muff' and isn't that social comment too – it certainly amused my son recently. Well it meant something entirely different in those days. Does the explanation – something that you put your hands in to keep them warm – make it better or worse?

The problem seems to be that no-one is particularly interested in the minutiae of their parents' or grandparents' or aunts' lives, until about thirty years after they have died, when unless you have special powers, it is too late to ask. If you have got special powers, or access to someone who has, you will be fine. It seems that these are just the sort of things 'spirits' like to share with us, so recourse to a psychic might do the trick.

"I've got a ... Mary here ... she says, yes she chipped that tea-pot ... the patterned one ... and she says get it valued, it might be valuable."

"Does the name John mean anything to anyone? ... I've got a John here, he wants his sister to know that he remembers her in that pink dress ... And ... Margaret? ... Dorothy ... is it ? ... Did you have a cat that got lost? You did? Well Granddad wants you to know that the cat is with him now, and very happy ... so not to worry."

Luckily they seem to like filling us in on such things, and not wasting our time with stuff about the afterlife.

But you don't need to go back so far, or look to the afterlife. Amazing changes are taking place right now, and perhaps we should be recording them. I started writing using a manual typewriter. Even when I had progressed to an electric typewriter, I still had to put in two sheets of paper, sandwiching a sheet of carbon paper. When you made the inevitable mistake that Tippex wouldn't obliterate (always at the bottom of the page) you had to rip it all out and start again. Now a click sorts everything. Recently I received a photograph taken on another continent, and sent from a mobile phone; whole process – 4 seconds. Not long ago that would have involved film, processing, mailing, and taken months. Typewriters and cameras can at least be preserved in museums. I'm already seeing examples of our past (and sometimes present!) possessions, appearing alongside pictures of dolly-tubs, and horse drawn carriages. But what of people's stories? They are just going to disappear. I have become a bit of a crusading 'write it down' bore. I know so many people with really interesting tales to tell but who aren't telling them, or haven't told them and are now dead. It is so sad.

A quick trawl around 'lost' stories in my own family brought up these.

The uncle by marriage who was abandoned by his mother together with his sister in a Liverpool park. They were found by someone, and taken to a children's home where they only saw each other through a fence. He then went on to captain a submarine in the war, was torpedoed, interned in an Italian prisoner of war camp – escaped – walked, living on tomatoes from the fields, until he met up with the allied forces. I know none of the details – he talked about it to me only once, and as far as I know, wrote nothing down. I saw only a piece in a newspaper about the torpedoing.

Amazingly, more abandoned children. An aunt by marriage, my husband's family this time, who left her two children – baby in pram, toddler holding on to pram handle, outside a shop; doubled out of the back door, leaving them there and going off with her lover. Here was a major con artist, who never told her third husband that she had been married twice before and had two children. Thirty? Forty? years later she traced these sons and surprisingly they managed to forgive her. Looking through old photos after she died the younger of them said –

"This is the woman who used to watch us in the street when we were children." He didn't of course know what his mother had looked like as a young woman. This brings me out in goose pimples. Mmm ... perhaps she wouldn't have wanted to write her story down.

I went with an aunt to Compton Verney. This is an impressive old house in 'Capability' Brown grounds that is fast becoming one of the country's top art venues. It has been beautifully restored and brought back to life at enormous expense, by Peter Moores of the Littlewood's football pools family of Liverpool. This aunt's father started a 'football pool' in Liverpool, but he made one fatal mistake – he used fixed odds. One dreadful Saturday, all the wrong teams won. My aunt remembers how all the family cowered under the table while people hammered on the doors and windows demanding their money. They had to sell their house to pay off their debts. Her father sold the business to the Moores family, and of course it became hugely profitable – hence the philanthropy. The weirdness of being in that house at Compton Verney, with her, just blew me away.

I could come up with more such stories from a very ordinary I would have thought, family. But what if nothing at all has happened in your family? Unlikely but possible.

I once read some memoirs of a woman I knew; she died in her eighties. She would have been the first to acknowledge that she had lived a very 'quiet' life. I don't think she ever left this country; her interests were nature and reading. She had described growing up in a small mining village in Warwickshire. Holidays were either with an aunt in Coventry – she described life in Coventry in the early 1900s; or with another aunt who lived in a village near Stratford-upon-Avon, a day long journey away by bus. She described roaming through the fields gathering wild flowers, the games they played, sweets they bought, her mother's poultices and herbal remedies. Surely this is interesting and important too?

I have discovered that social history is everywhere.

The 'Women's Register' that I mentioned earlier is a fascinating reflection of our changing times. It was originally called, 'Housewives' Register' for a start; how un-PC does that seem now? And it was formed because in the '50s there was nothing much for women at home with children. Plus women moved around a lot because of their husband's jobs, and it was difficult making new friends unless you wanted to just talk about children or baking. It was a sanity saver for me; somewhere to go and not talk about nappies, and other domestic trivia, things that were banned from the agenda. It was started by my friend of the China trip, and was such a revolutionary step forward for women's lives that she quite rightly got an OBE for the part she played in its formation. And if we are talking about stories to be told, how about this one for a hands down winner?

Her grandson studying The Women's Movement as part of his sixth form history course, saw her mentioned by name in his history book. He was able to put up his hand and say,

"That's my grandma." How wonderful is that?

Housewives' Register was hugely successful, its membership then being mostly young women with children, it is now mainly older women like me. Money was spent recently researching why membership was declining ... why? It is obvious. Life for women has changed out of all recognition in the last fifty years. Today's bright young mothers are out working, running businesses from home by computer, studying for Open University degrees, or training for charity marathons. They can get as much 'non domestic' input as they need and can cope with. I have just heard of a scheme for mothers, where they can breastfeed their babies while watching intelligent foreign films at the cinema during the day. There are better child care facilities, crèches practically from birth, play-schools, pre-schools, even some nurseries organised by employers.

Back to Women's Register – even in the minutiae of such an organisation is a history of social change.

We used to have coffee after the meeting. Everyone had coffee, because coffee in the '50s and '60s was young and trendy, and your parents, i.e. old people, all drank tea. Gradually as more people drank coffee, some members returned to tea which started becoming an 'in' drink again. Then awareness of caffeine crept in.

"Got any decaf?"

"What about cocoa – has that got caffeine?"

"Cocoa? You mean hot chocolate?"

Now it requires a pencil and paper and is a hostess's nightmare.

"Have you got camomile tea?"

"No – but I've got raspberry leaf."

"Mmmm ... don't like that. Have you got any of that, Fairtrade cranberry and mung bean?"

"Yes – next?"

"Just hot water for me – I've brought my own herbal 'night mixture' sachet."

Or my very favourite.

"I'll have coffee without the coffee please."

"... and that is ...?"

"Hot water with a dash of milk."

"Oh – OK."

Next?

"Tea without tea please."

"What is the difference between coffee without coffee and tea without tea?"

"She likes her coffee stronger than I like my tea."

I have never quite got my head round this. And what would our grandmothers have made of dozens of different sorts of bottled water, when we have perfectly good water on tap?

The changes are not just in drinking habits – they are in everything.

I see that a worried line of 'what to wear' anxiety, has wriggled its way through this narrative. That too has changed – not only the actual clothing, but also the importance of getting it right, and the ease with which you could get it wrong.

In the '50s I remember spending an uncomfortable evening at a rugby club social, wearing a sweater and skirt when all the other girls were wearing taffeta dance dresses. I wasn't going to make that mistake again at another rugby club social that I was invited to; so – low cut dress, starched petticoats, high heels, dangly earrings. This rugby club-house turned out to be a wooden hut in the middle of a muddy field where all the other girls, huddled round portable oil heaters, were wearing polo necks and woollen trousers. I suspect that jeans could be worn to both occasions now.

I have long since given up asking my American daughter-in-law what sort of clothes I should wear to this particular restaurant, or that social gathering. The answer was always the same. 'There is no dress code.' So unless you are actually traversing a red carpet, or black tie has been specified – anything goes, and whatever you wear nobody is going to raise an eyebrow. And what America decided yesterday...

My mother wore a large, lace-up, whalebone corset. We have certainly loosened our stays, literally and metaphorically, in my generation.

So, with only a minimum of fancy footwork I've managed to make this very satisfactory deduction. It's not just a catalogue of my mistakes. It's not just in case I get Alzheimers. It's not just for my children and grandchildren, or to give my friends a laugh – it's social history.

Thank goodness I've managed to justify my writing as something worthwhile. Clearly social history is very worthwhile – important, even.

So, what social history will my grandchildren's grandchildren, be interested in, looking back from the twenty second century?

"They travelled around in those funny tin box car things?... What? ... Along the ground?"

"And ... they carried babies around inside themselves ... for months! And they came out ..."

"Where!? ... Eugh!"

"... And they had them so young ... usually before they were sixty … I certainly don't intend to tie myself down with children till I'm at least ninety."

"Me neither … why would you even want to …?"

And it might not just be 'liver' that has them chewing their pencil equivalents.

"Marriage? How do you spell that?… What was it anyway?"

"I think it used to be something to do with the 'white dress' party … the one we have between living with someone, and it's getting a bit boring … and splitting up."

"Oh yes … you might be right … I've seen pictures … they definitely used to have the 'white dress' party."

And what will they think of my so exciting twentieth century travel experiences? Will someone say as I have just done,

"She lived a very quiet life … she never even left the planet."

I have just read about a travel club for women seeking women travel companions. A significant proportion of the members it seems are not single, widowed, or divorced, but married women who don't want to travel with their husbands. Presumably roughly equal numbers of their husbands don't want to travel with them. So I was not alone. It all catches up with you in the end.

And what about work? What jobs will they be doing? Will they still need bra designers, or will women all be fitted at puberty with those self-supporting grapefruit like implants, becoming popular even now, and thus negate the need for quick release fastenings, or studies in structural engineering? Will all farms have become paint balling centres, or plane parks for our private jets, and our food be shipped in from factories on some other planet? Will there be no wellingtons to fill, and arguments still raging about the distance that food has to travel?

"Three billion food miles is just too much! Why can't we grow it locally – in Australia?"

Will parents be able to choose some talents and a job to go with them, and get a chip directly implanted in their infant's brain? Save all the 'not knowing what you want to do' or thinking that you can do something when you can't.

What will my descendants think of my work experience?

"My great great grandmother worked on a newspaper ... no I don't know what it was either ... but she didn't seem to be very good at it." I think it was made of that 'paper' stuff that they used to use before computers. They mashed up trees into a pulp, and then dried it – in the sun probably.

"She built a house too ... of bricks ... clay I think they made them from ... they used to dig it out of the ground in the olden days ... build big fires ... and well ... burn it into lumps, and then stick them one on top of the other, to make some sort of shelter ... honestly ... can you imagine that our very own ancestors were so primitive?"

So there it is – it's social history – and it's important.

Well I've shown you mine, as the expression goes ... now show me yours.

More importantly – set it down for all those grandchildren's grandchildren of the twenty second century.